Asian Art

Volume III, Number 4   Fall 1990
Published by Oxford University Press
in association with the Arthur M. Sackler Gallery, Smithsonian Institution

...But a dream

Andrew H. Plaks

The literary convention of the dream journey as a short-lived passage from one state of being to another follows a pattern familiar to us from our everyday experience as nonliterary dreamers. We have all had the sensation of slipping away from the sure moorings of waking consciousness and drifting off toward a succession of uncertain images and scenes. The dream voyage may be as gentle as a rowboat gliding down a summer stream or as violent and wrenching as a great ship lurching through heavy seas. Either way, the visceral feeling of crossing a liminal barrier between two realms is inescapable. This feeling is probably among the few universals of human experience. Still, attempts to grasp its essence and to translate it into literary expression raise numerous questions regarding the destination of the dream passage and the meaning of the dreamer's eventual return.

Psychological and biological studies of the phenomenology of sleep and dreaming emphasize the threads of continuity between waking and dreaming modes of consciousness, perceiving them as two functional dimensions of a single psychic continuum.

Explanations of the entry into the dream and subsequent leaps by association often focus on somatic or kinetic stimuli—the triggering of dream responses by the fly, for example, buzzing in and out of Raskolnikov's dream at the end of part 3 of Fyodor Dostoyevski's *Crime and Punishment* (1866), or by the recalled sensation of a sleeping position in the opening discussion leading to the famous image of the taste of tea and madeleines that prompted Marcel Proust's (1871–1922) recapture of his past experience. At a more abstract level—but still within the domain of the physiological—dreams are frequently attributed to an excess of nervous energy built up during our waking hours and then released in the form of mental images. The related concept of dream as the concretization of desire, or wish fulfillment, tends to dominate our contemporary thinking on the subject. But it is important to remember that along with the vicarious gratification of elemental impulses, dreams may also incorporate into their very structure the inhibitions of the waking conscience.

The *Prose Poem of the Goddess*

Note: Chinese names are given surname first; handscrolls are read right to left.

Detail, *Second Red Cliff Prose Poem*. See figure 2d, page 63.

(Shennü fu), Han dynasty (206 B.C.– A.D. 220), offers a literary example, where the object of desire in an erotic dream is constrained by higher imperatives and suddenly vanishes, returning the dreamer abruptly to reality and to order.[1] On the other side of the physiological picture, dreamers and their chroniclers have long observed the quickening of heartbeat, raised body temperature, and other concrete manifestations of dream experience. In the writings of the Tang dynasty (618–907) Buddhist master Xuan Zang (596–664), for example, dream-induced involuntary sexual response is cited as proof of the material effects of the otherwise "empty" sphere of phenomenal existence.[2] A similar idea is expressed in innumerable dreams in fictional narrative, where it is almost obligatory for

the dreamer to continue feeling the pain, or pleasure, of dreamed experience after awakening. In all these examples, the underlying assumption is of an unbroken continuum taking in two linked phases, dreaming and waking consciousness, rather than an absolute cleavage between two separate states of being.

As in pictorial art, most literary representations of dreams, however, hinge on their discontinuity from waking reality. Sometimes this "otherness" is perceived as a difference more of degree than of kind, whereby dreams are invested with special aesthetic qualities that lift them out of the normal categories of experience. On the one side of the picture, it is the fuzzy or blurry quality of dreams, their Monet-like flickering images, that makes them feel conceptually separated from the distinct outlines of representationally perceived objects and events. This is often what renders them "dreamlike" in the first place. In other cases, the uniqueness of dream consciousness goes in exactly the opposite direction, toward greater vividness, with a sharper focus and more intense colors that make some dreams feel more real than real. One thinks, for example, of the wild thyme banks in William Shakespeare's *Midsummer Night's Dream* (1600) or, in the Chinese tradition, of the highly evocative garden settings for dream trysts in *The Peony Pavilion* (Mudan ting) by Tang Xianzu (1550–1616) and other classic dramas. One might even say that the keen sense of transience we experience in our dreams, both natural and literary, also sets them outside our normal perception of reality. What the Chinese and Japanese poets are fond of calling "dreams of springtime" tend to end just as they are starting to get good; they seem to dissolve into nothingness with an even greater rapidity than those moments of pure awareness we sometimes have in our waking lives.

The notion of separate orders of reality takes on greater force when dreams are distinguished from waking consciousness as truth from falsity. In literary examples, whether the dream is taken to be more true or more false depends very much on the narrative context and philosophical background against which it is woven. The "falseness" of dreams finds expression in a variety of religious and literary formulations. In the East Asian traditions, especially Buddhist and Daoist writings, images such as flowers in a mirror or the moon on the surface of

water frequently point to the illusory attachment of the unenlightened consciousness to external signs (although their use has subtle reverberations, for both of these symbols of insubstantiality actually reflect empirical reality). Moreover, such illusion often emerges as liberation from the containing strictures of gravity, sequential causality, and the like. In Chinese and Japanese fictional dreams, for example, it is no violation of the bounds of reason for the spirit of an imperial minister to take leave of his body, slay a dragon, and return unnoticed, all in the middle of a chess match; for a priest to enter the body of a golden carp and prevent the sin of taking the life of a sentient being; or for a young boy's soul to be transmuted into a fighting cricket in order to vindicate his filial devotion.[3]

In contrast, literary dreams may also be taken very seriously and invested with greater validity than the wakeful state, presented as vehicles of truth not expressible in ordinary forms of discourse. The dream as a medium of revelation is a staple of ancient and modern literatures. In the Mediterranean and European civilizations it appears as early as the epic of Gilgamesh (ca. 2000 B.C.) and forms a recurring pattern in the visions of the biblical patriarchs and prophets, although in both Jewish and Christian theology the prophetic dream is a lesser form of revelation than face-to-face communication with the Deity. There are numerous examples in later Western literature. In the early Chinese tradition admonitory and prophetic dreams occur in the *Zuozhuan* historical narratives attached to the canonic *Spring and Autumn Annals* (Chunqiu, ca. 5th century B.C.). Even in as undreamlike a text as the *Analects* (VII:5), Confucius provides an oblique affirmation of the efficacy of dreams as he bewails his troubling inability to conjure up the inspirational figure of the duke of Zhou. In Japanese literature nocturnal visions of karmic guilt and consequences abound, most memorably in Genji's encounter with his father's spirit while in exile at Suma, and in many Nō dramas of sin and expiation.

The dream as a privileged medium of communication reflecting deeper truth also lies at the heart of modern interpretations—Freudian, Jungian, and others—all of which hold that the symbolic language of dream provides a surer expression of psychic reality than the half-formed concepts of waking thought and speech. In literary criticism, archetypal symbols are also taken as keys to the interpretation of patterns of deep structure informing universal themes like desire and fulfillment, guilt and redemption.

In a number of important examples, the idea of dream as revelation of deeper truth is writ large and projected into a universal or cosmic vision. We can already see this impulse in the problematic twelfth tablet of the Gilgamesh narrative describing the monumental story of the god-king's rise and fall as a passing dream, or the biblical Jacob's dream of a ladder extending from earth to heaven. It becomes a major convention in the Greek and Latin classics, from the vision of the afterlife in the dream of Er in book 10 of Plato's *Republic* to Cicero's influential "Dream of Scipio," with its bird's-eye view of the structure of the cosmos and humankind's place within it. It is interesting that cosmic dream visions are apparently less common in Eastern traditions. In India, for example, the pervasive idea that the world is illusion undercuts the validity of universal revelation. In the Chinese and Japanese traditions, on the other hand, a relative disinterest in eschatology undercuts the importance of revelation. The dream as higher truth is thus a less fertile area for literary creativity.

In these traditions, therefore, the significance of literary dreams shifts from the revealed truth or unreality of the dream toward the meaning of the dreamer's awakening. One recurrent form is the tale of a hero whose entire lifetime passes before his eyes with all the powerful immediacy of lived experience, only to drop him abruptly into waking consciousness and show him, by one device or another, that time has virtually stood still in the interim. This is by no means an uncommon theme in world literature, occurring in various Islamic and medieval European versions.[4] In China this theme is best known in a whole series of classical tales. In one of these, "The World within a Pillow" (Zhenzhong ji, ca. eighth-century), a young man passes through yo-yo vicissitudes of glory and disgrace, bliss and pain, before waking to find his dinner still cooking on the stove. Here the return to reality carries with it a strong sense of *disillusionment*, a disburdening of the attachment to self that suggests at least the first steps toward enlightenment. Perhaps the most profound treatment of this theme in Chinese literature is found in the Tang tale "Du Zichun" (usually read in an expanded version in Feng Menglong's seventeenth-century story collection *Xingshi hengyan*).

In this powerful narrative a Job-like hero, subjected to an escalating series of horrors and suffering, is sustained by the promise of final enlightenment, only to succumb at the last moment to a remaining speck of elemental human compassion.

In all these cases, the awakening from the dream signifies the return of the dreamer to his original self—sadder or wiser, resigned to defeat or armed with a new spiritual insight. In certain other examples, however, the end of the dream journey is not a reversion to a prior state but an irreversible entry into a new phase of existence. This phase may, of course, simply mean drowning in a sea of illusion. Professor Anthony Yu has recently suggested, for example, that the placing of the dream revelation in *The Dream of the Red Chamber* (Hongloumeng) by Cao Xueqin (ca. 1715–1763) at the very beginning of the hero's passage through the garden of his youth means that he awakens not *out of* his prophetic afternoon nap but *into* the web of illusion that holds him and us for the rest of the book.[5]

The concept of final awakening into a new reality occurs in a more positive sense in a number of Asian texts. Zhuangzi (ca. 369–286 B.C.), for example, invokes the idea of a "great awakening" from the illusion of self, and a host of Buddhist sources speak of a true awakening from the mirage of ego-consciousness. The notion that the entire edifice of empirically perceived reality constitutes one grand dream, from which we are destined to awake sooner or later, is neither unique to Asian traditions nor unequivocal. It gives rise to conflicting interpretations regarding the ontological value of these interlocking states of being: What is real and what is not? One of the most common philosophical responses to the prospect of a final awakening is a kind of cosmic skepticism or, at least, existential doubt. In the Chinese tradition, the best-known example is Zhuangzi's dream of a butterfly, unable to determine whether the dreamer is dreaming the insect or the insect the dreamer. The conceit of the reversibility of subject-object, or dreamer-dreamed, occurs in Western texts as diverse as Plato's *Theaetetus* and Alice's dream of the Red King in Lewis Carroll's *Through the Looking Glass* (1872).[6] In Pedro Calderón's great seventeenth-century drama *La vida es sueño* it provides the philosophical core for the story of a prince deprived of his selfhood and finally unable to distinguish between illusion and reality, present and past. In certain Indian examples the denial of a clear boundary between dream and waking sometimes gives rise to an infinite regress, of detachment from reality followed by retranscendence from one's detached state, repeated endlessly. In other cases it may go no further than the expression of an unresolvable doubt. Zhuangzi's butterfly dream, after all, goes no further than saying that we cannot know. This is also the sense I get from the common Japanese figure of the "bridge of dreams"—a potential mediation between the world of the senses and ultimate reality that tends to be, as in a famous Shinkokin-shu poem, "snapped off," leaving us hanging in a limbo of indeterminacy.[7]

One easy philosophical "solution" to the question of whether we can or cannot know what is real is to sweep the ontological distinction between illu-

CHINA

sion and reality under the rug of one concept or another of transcendent unity. Zhuangzi's proverbial dream, for example, illustrates the Daoist idea of the "Nondifferentiation of Things" (*qiwu*). In literary expression, the idea of the identity of dreaming and waking consciousness is frequently pressed into service. For example, the great Nō dramatist and critic Zeami (1363–1443) appeals in a famous preface to the interchangeability of truth and illusion to account for the fine line

between existential anguish and ineffable awareness that forms the crux of his most powerful plays.

A Buddhist formulation of this idea current in Chinese literary texts is the opening section of the Prajnaparamita "Heart" sutra: "Form is no different from emptiness, emptiness is no different from form; form is identical to emptiness, emptiness is identical to form." Although the terms of this apparent tautology are not literally dream and waking, they are obviously related, so that one could almost paraphrase the statement as "la vida es sueño," or "life is but a dream." When we take a closer look, however, it is not altogether certain which of the two terms—"form" or "emptiness"—is closer to the dimension of consciousness we know as dream. Is it the illusory perception of reality expressed by the first term *se*, whose meaning ranges from "color" to "sensory perception" to "sensuality" to "sexuality"? Or is it the sister term *kong*, referring both to the literal void and other degrees of insubstantiality? The first half of this formula, telling us that the world of the senses is ultimately an illusion, is almost a commonplace of philosophical and literary expression. It is the converse, insisting that emptiness itself is equivalent to the illusion of form, that is more subtle and difficult to grasp.

For the most part, Chinese literary thinkers are content to leave the paradox of form and emptiness unresolved, allowing these two dimensions of being to coexist in a state of mutual implication in accordance with the time-honored conceptual model of complementary pairs associated with yin and yang. But this philosophical exercise of positing a complementary equivalence of form and emptiness, reality and illusion, is only taken up to a point. In China the idea of dream as the ultimate reality is invoked to undermine simpleminded faith in the world of appearances, but it rarely goes so far as to deny the ontological validity of the universe of experience. In other words, the complementary relation between illusion and truth, though theoretically a two-way street, usually has a logical direction. This is

especially true in the fictional representation of reality, in which frequent invocation of the philosophical notion of emptiness never fully abandons the convincing immediacy of the fabricated world. This notion is illustrated in perhaps the most thorough exploration of dream psychology in the Chinese tradition, the seventeenth-century novella *A Supplement to Journey to the West* (Xiyou bu) by Dong Yue (1620–1686). This dream-fantasy, as its title indicates, spins off from the sixteenth-century allegorical masterpiece *Journey to the West* (Xiyou ji) and then moves through a chain of episodes in the "Green-green World" (punning on the common sound—*qing*—of the words "green" and "desire"). In the end, however, the text pointedly returns to the reality of the original, fictional starting point, concluding with a line from the *Yijing*: "It informs and encompasses all the phenomena of Heaven and Earth; yet nothing goes beyond it."[8] The unbounded fantasy of the preceding dream journey is thus finally anchored within the coordinates of the existential universe.

If I may take as a final illustration a line neither intended nor perceived as a vehicle of philosophical profundity, I would like to read into the last verse of our most popular rhyme on dreams an example of the essential paradox of dream and reality. On the one hand, the idea that "life is but a dream" refers to "pure" dream, a momentary vision of undiluted perfection, blissfully detached from the world of pain and suffering. But at the same time, it cannot avoid being a "mere" dream, an illusory passage carrying us swiftly to the point of final reawakening.

Andrew H. Plaks is professor of East Asian studies at Princeton University. His publications include *Archetype and Allegory in the Dream of the Red Chamber* (1976), *Chinese Narrative: Critical and Theoretical Essays* (1977), and *The Four Masterworks of the Ming Novel* (1987), all published by Princeton University Press.

Notes

1. See Wai-yee Li, "Dream Visions of Transcendence in Chinese Literature and Paintings," in this issue.

2. Xuan Zang's discussion may be found in Feng Yu-lan, *A History of Chinese Philosophy*, trans. Derk Bodde (Princeton, N.J.: Princeton University Press, 1953), 2:323.

3. The first story is best known from its inclusion in the sixteenth-century novel *Journey to the West* (Xiyou ji), chap. 10. The second is found in the eighteenth-century Japanese collection *Ugetsu Monogatari*, trans. Leon Zolbrod (Vancouver: University of British Columbia, 1974), also translated by Kengi Hamada under the title *Tales of Moonlight and Rain* (New York: Columbia University Press, 1972). The third is the famous tale from the seventeenth-century Chinese collection *Liaozhai zhiyi* (Strange Tales from a Desultory Studio) by Pu Songling, widely known in the West in Lin Yutang's retelling entitled "Cricket Boy."

4. Some of these sources are reviewed in David R. Knechtges, "Dream Adventure Stories in Europe and T'ang China," *Tamkang Review* 4, no.2 (1973): 101–21.

5. Anthony C. Yu, "The Quest of Brother Amor: Buddhist Intimations in *The Story of the Stone*," *Harvard Journal of Asiatic Studies* 49, no.1 (1989): 55–92.

6. Some of these sources are discussed in Wendy D. O'Flaherty, *Dreams, Illusions, and Other Realities* (Chicago: University of Chicago Press, 1984), pp. 249 ff.

7. The poem, by Fujiwara no Teika (1162–1241), is translated and discussed by Robert H. Brower and Earl Miner in *Japanese Court Poetry* (Stanford, Calif.: Stanford University Press, 1961), p. 262.

8. The line occurs in the "Xici zhuan" (Commentary on the Attached Verbalizations) and can be found in *The I Ching*, trans. Richard Wilhelm (Princeton, N.J.: Princeton University Press, 1950), p. 296.

The Dream Journey in Chinese Landscape Art: Zong Bing to Cheng Zhengkui

Hongnam Kim

Cheng Zhengkui wished to paint five hundred handscrolls of the *Dream Journey* [among Rivers and Mountains] painting. Ten years ago I saw him as he reached the number three hundred. Some are several tens of feet long, some several feet long. Some are luxuriant, some simple; some are dark, some light. Each of them attained the highest perfection. But he valued his art so much that he was reluctant to give away his works to people except to the monk Shi.

—Zhou Lianggong, *Lives of Painters*, ca. 1672

More than twenty of Cheng Zhengkui's Dream Journey paintings have come down to us, their variety corresponding to Zhou Lianggong's description[1] (figs. 1–4). The seriousness and concentration with which Cheng Zhengkui carried out this extraordinary self-imposed task served as instruments for high artistic achievement. His persistent use of this single title reveals a personal outlook and motive; it also conveys a sort of manifesto. In Chinese history the term "dream journey" encompasses an immense corpus of ideas, particularly with respect to the relationship between humanity and nature. It is a fundamental principle governing Chinese landscape painting. In essence all Chinese landscape paintings are dream journeys.

An investigation of the dream journey in Chinese landscape painting begins with Zong Bing (375–443), the earliest recorded landscape painter of China, in whose biography in the *Song shu* (History of the Song Dynasty, ca. 420–479) the term "dream journey" appears. Guo Xi (after 1000–ca. 1090), a great eleventh-century landscapist, further refined the idea of the dream journey in his writings and works. In Cheng Zhengkui (1604–1676) and his Dream Journey series, the principle reached its culmination.

Zong Bing's Dream Journey

In *The Record of the Famous Painters of All the Dynasties* (Lidai minghua ji, completed 847), the ninth-century art historian Zhang Yanyuan (born ca. 815) speaks of Zong Bing as the first

Figure 1. Cheng Zhengkui, *Dream Journey among Rivers and Mountains*, no. 30, 1674, Qing dynasty. Handscroll, ink and color on paper, 69³/₄ × 9¹/₈ in. The Metropolitan Museum of Art, Gift of Harry Lenalt, 1955

recorded painter of landscapes and preserves Zong's treatise "Preface to Landscape Painting" (Hua shanshui xu, ca. 433–43). Zong is described as a highly learned aesthete and recluse who excelled in painting, calligraphy, and music. He loved nature and constantly traveled to famous mountains. In fact Zong is known to have lived on Mount Heng (in Hunan), one of the Five Sacred Mountains of China. When he became too old and sick to climb, he covered the walls of his room with his own paintings of his beloved mountains. According to Zhang Yanyuan, Zong Bing said: "Alas, old age and illness have arrived together, and I fear that I can no longer roam the famous mountains everywhere. I can purify my heart and behold the Way only by roaming the mountains while lying down."[2] "Roaming the mountains while lying down" is a literal translation of *woyiyouzhi* (*woyou* in short), which is poetically rendered "dream journey." This appears to be the first use of the term, and thereafter it was always associated with Zong Bing.

Zong Bing's "Preface to Landscape Painting" is the earliest treatise on the subject in China, and probably in the

world for that matter. It envisages an intricate web of ideas and concepts—philosophical and pictorial—that would be fundamental to the aesthetics of Chinese landscape art. On the pictorial and technical level, Zong introduced the idea of the painted image as a substitute for the actual. Relating his discovery of landscape painting with enthusiasm and excitement, Zong expressed, in the words of a modern scholar, a "sense of wonder at the artist's ability to bring a vast expanse of landscape within the bounds of his picture"[3]. He exclaimed, "A vertical stroke of three inches equals a height of several thousand feet, and a horizontal passage of ink over a few feet stands for a distance of a hundred miles."

Zong Bing argued, however, that painted landscape can successfully substitute for the real only when verisimilitude is achieved along with the spiritual animation of what is depicted:

If one considers it a natural course that response by the eye causes the mind to accord, that means when similitude is skillfully achieved [in painting], eyes will also respond completely and the mind be entirely in accord. This response by the eye

and accord by the mind to painting will move the spirit and, as the spirit soars, the truth will be attained. Even though one should again futilely seek out remote cliffs, what more could be added? The divine spirit, which is essentially limitless, resides in forms and stimulates all kinds of life, and truth enters into reflections and traces [i.e., painting]. One who can truly depict things skillfully will also attain the truth.

To Zong, the painted images of mountains on his walls functioned as substitutes for the actual mountains he could no longer visit. "Roaming the mountains while lying down" was a conscious act of imagination by which he transported himself to the mountains in order to reengender the state of body and mind induced by being in nature. Zong believed, as did many of his contemporaries, that the potency of the mountains enabled him to "concentrate my vital energies and attune my body," thereby sustaining his physical and spiritual well-being. In other words, his transposition of the potency inherent in the natural order to the man-made order made it possible for painted landscape to substitute for the real.

On the philosophical level, Zong's concept of the dream journey revolved around thoughts and practices that not only governed his time but also became the underlying inspiration for all ages of Chinese landscape painting. These ideas include Daoism in both its philosophical and popular religious forms; a cosmological, binary (yin and yang) understanding of the universe; the practice of eremitism as a valid lifestyle and method of political protest; ascetic Confucianism; the idealization of antiquity, as in the Yao-Shun myth of the golden age; and the act of producing and appreciating paintings as ritual. The idea of the dream journey also shares the abundant romanticism of nature poetry in Zong's day.

The following statement from Zong Bing's treatise is critically important in this regard:

I long for [the mountains] Lu and Heng, am cut off from [the hills of] Jing and Wu: I had not realized that old age is coming on. I am ashamed that I cannot concentrate my vital energies and attune my body. . . : so now I draw pictures, spread colors, and build up these cloud-capped ranges.

And so it is that I live at leisure and control my vital breath, wipe clean my wine-cup and strum my lute, unroll my paintings in seclusion, and sit contemplating the four corners of the world. I do not oppose

Figure 2 (above and below).
Cheng Zhengkui, *Dream Journey among Rivers and Mountains*, no. 90, 1658, Qing dynasty. Handscroll, ink and color on paper, 135$^{1}/_{2}$ × 10$^{1}/_{4}$ in. The Cleveland Museum of Art, Purchase, Mr. and Mrs. William H. Marlatt Fund, 1960

the celestial influences, but in my loneliness respond to the unpeopled wilderness, where peaks and precipices rise to soaring heights, [clothed in] their vast clouds and forests.

Zong Bing inherited the belief that "mountains and waters"—in Chinese *shanshui*, the word for "landscape"—are the noblest manifestation of the Dao, the ultimate truth that regulating, self-renewing laws are innate to all things and accord with each other. He was probably the first artist to apply this highly abstract and almost mystical understanding to art. Zong's transposition of the spiritual energy from the nature to the painting order made it possible for the viewer to take a dream journey, that is, to transform his mental state from the secular to the spiritual and, being fully in communion with the spirits of the mountains and valleys, achieve an intuitive understanding of the Dao. Zong was profoundly affected by the mystical writings of his period such as the "Neipian," a famous treatise on alchemy and herbalism of the elixirs of immortality written by the Daoist Ge Hong (ca. 280–340). Typical of his time, Zong Bing wedded this mystic experience of the Dao at its highest level with the attainment of immortality. He believed in the practice of religious Daoism and the cult of mountain immortals as a means to nourish the spirit and harmonize the body with the forces of nature, finally accomplishing the extension of the life span into immortality.[4]

Although Zong Bing did not elaborate upon the eremitic aspect of his life and thought, evidence abounds that in his day eremitism was a strong undercurrent with implications of political censure, asceticism, and idealism. A recluse himself, Zong Bing refused to take a government position in order to pursue a simple life away from the mundane world. Many of the personages mentioned in his "Preface to Landscape Painting" were ancient recluses and hermits whom he emulated all his life, and he made numerous pilgrimages to the mountains with which these ancient sages were associated.

Wo, the first character of the term *woyou* (dream journey), often refers to the idea of withdrawal from the world. Examples abound: *womingli* means "to cease [*wo*] from the pursuit of fame [*ming*] and wealth [*li*]"; *wolung* (sleeping dragon) refers to a great man in retirement who is yet to be discovered; *gaowo* (to sleep high) refers to a lofty man who has retired from the cares of public life in peace and safety; *woyun* (to make clouds one's bed) means to live the life of the hermit; *woxue* (to stay at home while it is snowing) means to retreat when the world is in trouble—the behavior of a man of integrity and superiority.[5] Therefore, the word *wo* as a politico-philosophical metaphor for recluse is embedded in Zong's concept of the dream journey.

Eremitism was the most accepted means of political protest and social criticism throughout the history of

Figure 2. Detail

mitism, renouncing the mundane and denouncing the current political and social situation. Both desired to evoke the life of natural and high-minded simplicity that they thought had existed in times past.

This last element—the desire to return to antiquity—is a basis for the most enchanting dream to ever console the Chinese (perhaps all humankind): the myth of a golden age ruled by two legendary kings, Yao and Shun, when people lived on the fruits of the earth peacefully, piously, and in primitive simplicity. This dream of the golden age is evoked in every major philosophical and historical writing of traditional China. Tao Qian's poetry is essentially a look backward, with longing, at that idealized antique world with all its fullness of life and confidence.

Eremitism also has an ascetic imperative, which exerted a strong but covert influence over the structure of Chinese Confucian and Daoist philosophy, ethics, and aesthetics. The life of a recluse was to be led in the most simple manner possible, with the utmost emotional restraint, at the most humble location, and in the meanest abode, where one would not be distracted by anything mundane. Only such environs and attitudes could provide the decorum and emotional control that one needed to achieve tranquillity, the ultimate goal of which is eloquently stated by Jia Yi (201–169 B.C.) in his famous poem "The Owl" (Fu niao fu):

A true man is tranquil
And rests alone with the Truth,
Renouncing intellect and spurning
   material things,

China. Zong Bing was born in the "unfortunate" time of disunion, the Southern Dynasties (317–589), when the northern part of the empire was ruled by "barbarians." Numerous contenders laid violent claim for heaven's mandate to rule, and good fortune one day was the source of disaster the next. The most eloquent expression of the eremitic spirit of Zong's time is found in the poetry and prose of the contemporaneous poet-recluse Tao Qian (365–427), which takes the reader on a kind of dream journey to the ideal world of antiquity, as seen in his famous "Record of the Peach Blossom Spring" (Taohuayuan ji, ca. 397–405).

Tao's pastoral world and poetic journey contrast with Zong's alpine world and pictorial journey, yet they share a strong element of naturalism—be it profane or spiritual. Both inspired the rise of landscape painting. Recluses from the world, they believed in ere-

Remaining aloof and unconcerned for himself,
He roams at will in the infinite with the Truth.[6]

The final line of this poem expresses the core of Zong Bing's concept of dream journey, the ultimate goal of which is attaining truth through landscape painting, the "images of the mind": "This response by the eye and accord by the mind to painting will move the spirit and, as the spirit soars, the truth will be attained."

To Zong, his dream journey was an act of ritual in his ascetic and solitary pursuit of sagehood and immortality: "I live at leisure and control my vital breath, wipe clean my wine cup and strum my lute, unroll my paintings in seclusion, and sit contemplating the four corners of the world." How striking is it to find these words repeated verbatim by the great masters Shen Zhou (1427–1509) and Gong Xian (1619–1689) and expressed in the attitude of Cheng Zhengkui! The repetition has an intensity, a total seriousness, that recalls religious conversion especially in the use of an idiosyncratic formula to attain an internal reward. The preparation for unrolling the paintings, as Zong describes it, is a ritual process—nearly like self-hypnosis or meditation—that would help strip the mind of outside concerns and create a setting conducive to total absorption. Zong, then, transcends himself and experiences a heightened awareness of his being when he enters into a private dialogue with his landscapes.

Zong Bing's concept of woyou provided a powerful beginning for Chinese landscape painting. From its very inception the art of landscape was considered inseparable from spiritual life. Furthermore, by introducing the idea of woyou, Zong contributed to the creation of China's enduring myths of mountains and rivers and to the awakening of the imaginative faculty, setting in the early Chinese mind a basic pattern for the tastes and attitudes of future scholars who would develop the idea of the "mind landscape."

Guo Xi's *Early Spring*: Dream Journeys from the Real to the Ideal

Following Zong Bing, no Chinese artist or critic considered recording a true visual impression of nature to be an end sufficient in itself. Landscape had to carry with it qualities of poetry, spirituality, and philosophy. The quest for a means of expressing these qualities was preceded by the establishment of a visual vocabulary and techniques to achieve outward likeness. This step was followed by a "reconstruction" of nature into an ideal form by means of selected motifs. Whether lyrical or prosaic, the artist's intent was that of a "poetic portrait." Simultaneously Chinese art moved toward capturing the essence of the depicted in its purest and the most concentrated form, beyond what the eye merely perceives. The ultimate goal was not only to create a likeness of the physical world but to present mountain landscape as a microcosm of the universe that would evoke in both artist and viewer not only the intuitive understanding of the natural order, Dao, but also the awareness of the correspondence between natural phenomena and human life. The first great breakthrough in these developments occurred in the monumental mountain landscape painting of the Five Dynasties (907–960) and the Northern Song (960–1127) periods. The advent of these pictorial idealizations of objective reality marked the beginning of landscape as the major force of Chinese art.

Early Spring, painted in 1072 by one of the great eleventh-century masters, Guo Xi, epitomizes these endeavors (fig. 5). A work that balances the ideal and the real, it displays technical mastery and great refinement in pictorializing a panoramic view of mountains, valleys, and streams with scattered figures of fishermen and woodcutters and a Buddhist monastery. Mountain peaks rise and fall through unbroken ranges into the far distance, veiled here and there by mist and clouds. Composed in a vertical format with multiple perspectives, twists and turns, and flat distances, it breaks the boundaries of the fixed-vantage-point perspective and allows the viewer to take a journey through nature with the artist.

Guo Xi was the most eloquent spokesman of his time. In his famous essay "The Lofty Message of Forest and Streams" (Linquan gaozhi), he pointed out, "If you survey present-day scenery, in a hundred miles of land to be settled, only about one out of three places will be suitable for wandering and living."[7] He believed landscape painting should depict only that rare place of beauty most desirable for "wandering" and "living." *Early Spring* is a composite of selected, realistically rendered motifs—writhing peaks, distinguished-looking pine trees, a picturesque waterfall and a monastery, veils of vapor and mist. These elements are idealistically reassembled into an imaginary landscape. The painting stands as the powerful statement of an artist determined to improve upon the surrounding world.

Guo Xi further believed that a painting had to evoke a mood, not merely depict scenery. In his essay he noted, "To look at a particular painting puts you in the corresponding mood . . . the corresponding frame of mind as though you were really on the point of going there. This is the wonderful power [*miao*] of a painting beyond its mere mood." He affectionately described the evocative character of each season's atmosphere: "clouds and vapors . . . are genial in spring, profuse in summer, sparse in autumn, and somber in winter . . . mists and haze

Figure 3. Cheng Zhengkui, *Dream Journey among Rivers and Mountains*, no. 25, 1652, Qing dynasty. Handscroll, ink and color on paper, 120 × 10¹/8 in. The Palace Museum, Beijing

. . . on spring mountains are gently seductive and seem to smile." Chinese landscape painting was moving ever closer to poetry, the art of evocation and sympathetic resonance.

In the same essay Guo Xi refreshed and elaborated Zong Bing's idea of dream journey to suit the landscape art of his own era:

In what does a gentleman's love of landscape consist? The cultivation of his fundamental nature in rural retreats is his frequent occupation. The carefree abandon of mountain streams is his frequent delight. The secluded freedom of fishermen and woodsmen is his frequent enjoyment. The flight of cranes and the calling of apes are his frequent intimacies. The bridles and fetters of the everyday world are what human nature constantly abhors. Immortals and sages in mists and vapors are what human nature constantly longs for and yet is unable to see. It is simply that, in a time of peace and plenty, when the intentions of ruler and parents are high-minded, purifying oneself is of little significance and office-holding is allied to honor. Can anyone of humanitarian instinct then tread aloof or retire afar in order to practice a retreat from worldly affairs? And, if so, will he necessarily share the fundamental simplicity of [legendary recluses such as Hsü Yu, associated with] Mount Chi and the River Ying, or participate in the lingering renown of [the Han dynasty's] Four Old Men of Mount Shang? Their songs, such as the "Ode to

the White Pony" and the "Hymn to the Purple Fungus," are of what has passed away and is unattainable. But, are the longing for forests and streams, and the companionship of mists and vapors, then to be experienced only in dreams and denied to the waking senses?

It is now possible for subtle hands to reproduce them in all their rich splendor. Without leaving your room you may sit to your heart's content among streams and valleys. The voices of apes and the calls of birds will fall on your ears faintly. The glow of the mountain and the color of the waters will dazzle your eyes glitteringly. Could this fail to quicken your interest and thoroughly capture your heart? This is the ultimate meaning behind the honor which the world accords to landscape painting. If this aim is not principal and the landscape is approached with a trivial attitude, it is no different from desecrating a divine vista and polluting the clear wind.

I have quoted this passage at length because it demonstrates the extent to which earlier beliefs, attitudes, and critical vocabulary are perpetuated and influence art. Guo Xi clearly evokes Zong Bing and repeats Zong's dictum of the dream journey—that when good painters make successful renditions of real landscape, "without leaving your room you may sit to your heart's content among streams and valleys" and be put in "the corresponding frame of mind as though you were

Figure 4. Detail, Cheng Zhengkui, *Imaginary Journey among Streams and Mountains*, no. 150, 1661, Qing dynasty. Handscroll, ink and color on paper, 210¼ × 14⅛ in. Los Angeles County Museum of Art, Far Eastern Art Council Funds

really on the point of going there." Guo concluded that it is for this quality of response that landscape art receives the highest favor and honor.

Changes in art are affected by both internal and external forces. Once the meaning and symbolism of a chosen subject are established, they become self-evident. From that point artists pursue issues inherently aesthetic; their techniques and ideas are inevitably affected by their times. At a certain point Chinese painting began to follow its own internal laws. Although individual genius occasionally provided a new direction, over the long term the minds of artists and theorists remained governed by the fundamental assumptions of the dream journey. So implicit were these assumptions that even titles became insignificant appendages. The idea of the dream journey firmly in place, landscape painters of China directed their efforts toward the creation of the most ideal world and the most ideal dream journey. In the process of viewing, as in the process of making, one experienced a heightened

awareness of being, one entered into a private dialogue with the imagery and achieved a state of perfect, powerful absorption. Through this mystic communion, landscape painting thus became almost iconic, a vehicle of "ritual."

Cheng Zhengkui's *Dream Journey among Rivers and Mountains*

Cheng Zhengkui was a renowned scholar-painter active in the southern city of Nanking in the mid-seventeenth century.[8] Of the five hundred landscapes called *Dream Journey among Rivers and Mountains*, more than twenty survive, all inscribed with this title and numbered[9] (see figs. 1–4). The paintings are horizontal scrolls approximately nine to fourteen inches high, some stretching nearly twenty feet. They present a long narrow horizontal strip of distant scenery, with little establishment of foreground or visual reference to a fixed position of

artist and viewer. Everything is set down in the same clarity of focus.

The typical scenery is a refined yet elusive "Shangri-la" created from a limited number of carefully selected motifs—rustic huts, choice grass, grouped trees, undulating hills, and mountains. These seemingly ordinary sights are magnetically charged by Cheng's personal interpretation and artistic expression. In a rarefied environment, phantomlike figures—not rustic woodcutters and fishermen but men of gentle class and demeanor— roam about at leisure as if safely ensconced in their family estates. The scene becomes increasingly unrealistic when we discover garden rocks set in the middle of nowhere, as in the case of the Los Angeles County Museum of Art handscroll (see fig. 4). In such a world "reality" becomes entirely a dynamic interplay of suggestive imagery.

Deft and economical of both ink and brush, often devoid of color, most Dream Journey paintings have the effect of snowy landscapes—a kind of winter poetry. Gong Xian admired this aspect of Cheng's painting, describing it as "like a man of icy flesh [cool appearance] and jade bones [lofty character]; thus it is like the calligraphy of Master Dong Qichang from Huating."[10] Gong Xian's comparison of Cheng's painting to the calligraphy of Dong Qichang (1559–1636), with whom Cheng had in fact studied, was probably made to point out Cheng's stoic, quintessential approach to forms—their angularity and linear clarity. With a sense of purpose and confidence in composition, Cheng

Figure 4. Detail

樹杪黃葉溪
澗凍搖閬仙
居家上願不
藉物挑澗甃
微甚山早見
氣如蒸
己卯春月
尚題

Figure 5. Guo Xi, *Early Spring*, 1072, Song dynasty. Hanging scroll, ink and color on silk, 62^1/$_4$ × 42^5/$_8$ in. The National Palace Museum, Taiwan, Republic of China

used brush and ink to create forms that are seemingly conventional and repetitive. But, reaching beyond timid reliance on stylistic convention, which would have sunk a lesser painter into the depths of triviality and mediocrity, he worked these forms, pulling them apart and reassembling them with virtuosity and devotion. The painting, by its intense concentration and ritual precision, compels us.

What had happened to Chinese

landscape painting since Guo Xi? What was it that made Cheng Zhengkui no longer content to assemble the precious fragments of nature into a lifelike whole? What made him paint in such an intellectual, abstract, and detached manner? Why did Cheng impose on himself the extraordinary task of painting five hundred handscrolls of landscape with the single title, *Dream Journey*?

Cheng Zhengkui's Dream Journey paintings appear to have a multilayered meaning when we try to answer these questions against his life, his artistic background, and his times. Cheng wrote on a Dream Journey painting dated 1652:

There are three difficulties to living in Changan [Beijing]: there are no mountains and rivers to enjoy, no calligraphy and painting to study, no collectors from whom I can borrow. Therefore I decided to produce a hundred scrolls of *Dream Journey among Rivers and Mountains* to be circulated [in substitute of the real] in order to save those friends who are in service. I have completed so far about thirty scrolls, all of which have been taken away by the art-lovers, except this scroll which I now inscribe and present to Wugong.

On another Dream Journey painting, dated 1659, he inscribed:

[My friend] Gongyuan said to me that my river scenery does not look natural. I said: "Since the creative energy of the universe is in my palm, I should be able to open a new world. Why should I be dependent on the left-over water and disheveled mountains? Moreover, seas, hills, and valleys are like blue dogs and white clouds; a thousand years are like a blink of moment. Who knows, someday rivers and mountains may move into my painting?"[11]

The notions in these two inscriptions flesh out much of Zong Bing's original concept of the dream journey, particularly the idea of landscape painting as the substitute for real landscape and as an expression of eremitism. Cheng Zhengkui evoked Zong Bing to reassert the spiritual values with which men of antiquity endowed the art of landscape and to recall those essentials that were often obliterated in the course of history. Both Cheng and Zong Bing lived in periods of despair over the onslaught of foreign invasions that tore the country apart. In such times, retirement and withdrawal were the prevailing mode of life among intellectuals and artists.

Cheng was born in 1604 into the Confucian environment of high Ming society. He was a member of the scholar elite, a most prestigious and affluent status secured almost exclusively through passing civil examinations. Following the footsteps of his father, who was a vice-minister in the Ministry of Revenue, Cheng received a *jinshi* (doctorate) degree and was honored by an appointment to the prestigious Hanlin Academy in 1631. Destined for a carefully articulated and consciously shaped way of life, he became a typical scholar-official-gentleman, with the leisure time and means to sustain the aesthetic life.

But in the catastrophic year 1644 the native Ming dynasty crumbled under the Manchus, who would rule China into the modern era. The dynastic fall was a calamity for Confucian scholar-officials, both active and retired, as well as for all degree holders and intellectuals. Each had to make the agonizing decision, often at great personal cost, whether to uphold the strict Confucian doctrine of *zhong* (loyalty to the

Figure 6. Huang Gongwang, *Dwelling in the Fuchun Mountains*, 1350, Yuan dynasty. Handscroll, ink on paper, 251 × 12¹/8 in. The National Palace Museum, Taiwan, Republic of China

ruler) or to become a collaborator by serving the Manchus. Many chose to remain loyal to the Ming court by committing suicide, joining a resistance army, or forsaking the world as a monk or a hermit. Many also chose to serve. Whatever the choice, all were victims of war, history, and the Confucian institution of loyalism.

Little of Cheng's personal situation is known until 1649, when he finally chose to serve the Manchu court. Probably he realized that the mandate of the Ming court was gone, and his commitment to public service compelled him to continue working for his country and his people. Moreover, outright refusal to serve the Manchus would also bring about a different sort of calamity—an indictment for treason. For the next eight years Cheng was a high official, reaching the posi-

tion of vice-minister in the Ministry of Works. He lived in retirement from 1657 until his death in 1676.

Political involvement, avoided at peril, was at the same time tainted by danger. The dense air of Beijing was unsettling, with intense political uncertainty and complexity that threatened personal security. Conscious of his graceless conformity to circumstances beyond his control, Cheng was probably even more pained by having to serve at the capital, the very center of the Manchu empire. He produced his first Dream Journey painting in 1649, the year he took up his position at court. In such an environment, the evocation of the dream journey was more than simple, poignant nostalgia. Cheng painted dream journeys "in order to save those friends who are in service" and, more important, himself.

He had to paint dream journeys to
alleviate the sense of adversity and
spiritual unres. he and others deeply
felt. Further, with their many layers of
ancient significance—particularly that
of eremitism—the paintings were a
means of political protest. Though
many of Cheng's writings are largely
complimentary in tone, to the point of
concealing much of his inner turmoil,
occasionally his emotional constraint
is betrayed, as the phrase "left-over
water and disheveled mountains" in
his inscription suggests. Such images
were used frequently by native Chinese
of strongly loyalist sentiment to refer
to the state of their country, now over-
run by the "barbarians."

As Kenneth J. DeWoskin has
observed, "Involvement with the arts
identified one, for others and oneself
as well, as part of the enduring order

and motion of nature, and created at
least a semblance of shelter from the
hazards and transience of political life.
The literatus, enmeshed in worldy
affairs at the court, . . . in [the arts]
finds solace and momentary seclusion."[12] To undertake the act of landscape painting was to assert the higher
values of apolitical living, mental com-
posure, and personal comfort in the
natural world—motivation rooted in
an actual life of very opposite condi-
tions. The aesthetic life, with its
intense concentration upon the art of
landscape painting and accompanying
ideology of the dream journey, was a
means of both escape and liberation.

Cheng's repetition of the dream
journey theme bears an aura of religious fervor akin to the Buddhist
practice of copying sutras for contem-
plation and salvation. To Cheng, the

execution of the Dream Journey paintings, each with the utmost sincerity and intensity, was indeed a ritual. In a time of rage, betrayal, grief, loss, futility, agony—all of which must have been so immediate and palpable—Cheng was seeking emotional equilibrium. Disgusted by reality, he desired reflection and quiet dialogue with the cathedral of nature constructed in his mind, as is possible only in dreams. Painting was also a process of self-cultivation and an attempt to live concretely the life of the perfected Confucian. Cheng was one of those Confucians Theodore de Bary describes as "both supremely atypical and ideally normative. In the sense that he was an extremist in his exacting fulfillment of ritualized life, he was atypical; and in the sense that his extremism represented the natural extension of Confucian precepts, he was normative." Indeed, as John A. Hay has commented, "Landscape painting (so is the miniature garden) was part of a closely woven fabric of immortality, mountain-dwelling, the scholar's studio and the perfection of the humanistic self."[13]

Also critical to our understanding of Cheng's Dream Journey paintings and implicit in his writings is the notion of the artist not as mere imitator but as creator of a world "truer than real." Cheng received this important precept from his famous teacher Dong Qichang, who wrote in "Discussions on Painting" (Huashuo), "The Dao of painting is to hold the universe in your hand." This internalization of natural landscape, molding it to individual visual language, had become the creative force in Chinese pictorial art from

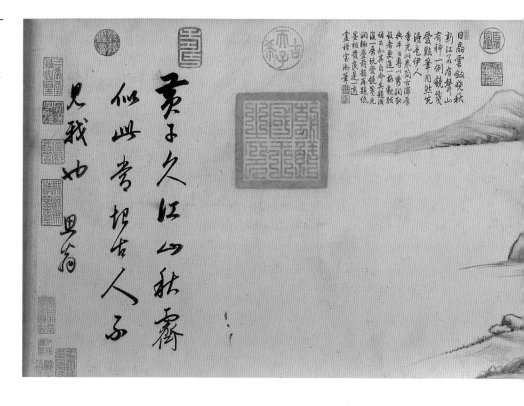

Figure 7. Dong Qichang, *Autumn Mountains*, ca. late 16th–early 17th centuries, Ming dynasty. Handscroll, ink on paper, 537/8 × 151/8 in. The Cleveland Museum of Art, Purchase from the J. H. Wade Fund

the Yuan dynasty (1279–1368) onward. Ni Zan (1301–1374), a great landscapist of that period, scorned technical procedures and had only contempt for those who judged a picture by its "likeness." Criticized for not achieving verisimilitude, he said proudly: "It is not given to everyone to achieve the absence of likeness."[14]

The pictorial solution for such a relentless quest came from the belief that the spirit of landscape can be captured in formal structure and brushwork rather than in the imitation of real landscape. This solution has, as May Anna Quan Pang has pointed out, "philosophical import in portraying the hierarchical order of the Universe and the principle of change in the constant transformation of formal relationships throughout the landscape."[15] This constructive mode of

landscape painting began to take discernible shape in the works of the Yuan masters, as represented by Huang Gongwang's (1269–1354) *Dwelling in the Fuchun Mountains* (fig. 6), the quintessential literati painting of China. It communicates the artist's creative energy through the kinesthetic portrayal of nature. Landscape painting further evolved to structuralism and nature-derived abstractionism in the works of Dong Qichang (fig. 7). All the leading painters of Cheng's century were directly or indirectly influenced by the Yuan masters and Dong. As an esteemed student of Dong Qichang and an ardent follower of the Yuan masters, particularly Huang Gongwang, Cheng sums up their legacy in his paintings.

The fundamentalism and the ontology in Cheng's art was in fact shared

by two of the century's foremost painters, Gong Xian and Shitao. Gong Xian believed in the ability of the artist's creative force to break open the state of *hundun* (amorphousness) in all existence and provide order. Shitao (1641–ca. 1720) returned to the very creative impulse of life in his works and in his treatise "Record of Sayings about Painting" (Huayu lu). In his quest to create landscape painting, so perfect and so self-evident, he did not need to turn to nature; truth, he believed, was written and engraved in the painted image. Cheng's words, as well as his works, manifest perfectly Dong Qichang's clearly drawn distinction between art and nature: "For the rare wonders of scenery, painting is no equal to mountains and water; but mountains and water are no equal to painting for the sheer marvels of brush and ink."

Cheng Zhengkui's Dream Journey paintings express, in his own most sparing manner, his innermost feeling and aesthetic conviction. They are the culmination of Chinese aesthetic pursuits, the fundamentals of which are found in Zong Bing's concept of the dream journey: artlessness, minimalism, reticence, *pingdan* (placidity), stoicism, and eremitism. The dream journey the reclining Zong Bing wished to take through his landscape paintings was to the sacred mountains and valleys that existed in objective reality. In contrast, Cheng Zhengkui's dream journey paintings stand as the ideal landscape of subjective reality, the landscape of the enlightened mind. Cheng's dream journey ends in his creation of nature, his own dream world. To him the act of painting was a way of life, a ritual and a means to pursue his ideal of the perfected man.

Hongnam Kim is curator of the Rockefeller Collection of Asian Art, the Asia Society, New York. She received her doctorate from Yale University in Chinese art history. She has published on Chinese and Korean painting, calligraphy, and ceramics.

Notes

1. Zhou Lianggong, *Duhua lu*, 4 juan (ca. 1672), in *Yishu congbian*, comp. Yang Jialo (Shanghai: Shijie shuju, 1968), trans. Hongnam Kim, in "Chou Liang-Kung and His *Tu-hua-lu* (Lives of Painters): Patron-Critic and Painters of Mid-Seventeenth Century China" (Ph.D. diss., Yale University, 1985), 2:78.

2. Zhang Yanyuan, *Lidai minghua ji*, in *Yishu congbian*, 1962 ed., 6:207–11, trans. William Acker, in *Some T'ang and Pre-T'ang Texts* (Leiden: E. J. Brill, 1974), 2:115–22. Zong Bing's "Preface to Landscape Painting" is also translated by Michael Sullivan, *The Birth of Landscape Painting in China* (Berkeley: University of California Press, 1962), pp. 102–3, and by Susan Bush and Hsiao-yen Shih, *Early Chinese Texts on Painting* (Cambridge, Mass.: Harvard-Yenching Institute, 1985), pp. 36–38.

3. Sullivan, *Birth of Landscape Painting in China*, p. 102. All subsequent quotations from Zong Bing's preface are from Sullivan's translation, with the author's modifications.

4. See Jerome Silbergeld, "Chinese Concepts of Old Age and Their Role in Chinese Painting, Painting Theory, and Criticism," *Art Journal* 46, no. 2 (1987): 103–14.

5. Tetsui Morohashi, comp., *Dai kanwa jiten* (Tokyo: Daishu kan shoten, 1955–60), 9:388.

6. Jia Yi, "The Owl," in *Anthology of Chinese Literature from Early Times to the Fourteenth Century*, ed. Cyril Birch (New York: Grove Press, 1965), 1:138–40.

7. Guo Xi, "The Lofty Message of Forest and Streams," trans. Bush and Shih, *Early Chinese Texts on Painting*, pp. 150–54, 156–58, 160–62, 165–69, 177–82, 187–88. All subsequent quotations from Guo Xi's essay are from this translation.

8. See Yang Xin, *Cheng Zhengkui* (Shanghai: Renmin Meishu Chubanshe, 1982).

9. The assigned numbers appear to be neither consecutive nor chronological within a given year; numbers 20 and 180, for example, were both done in 1670. Cheng's writings and numbering pattern suggest that he probably painted a series of scrolls, often one hundred but sometimes two or three hundred per set, each series completed in some arbitrary self-imposed time limit of one or two years.

10. Gong Xian, quoted in Kim, "Chou Liang-kung and His *Tu-hua-lu*," vol. 3, "Catalogue of Extant Paintings Dedicated to Chou Liang-kung," entry 2, pp. 10–11.

11. Cheng Zhengkui, inscriptions quoted in Yang Xin, "Cheng Zhengkui ji chi 'Jiangshan woyou tu,'" *Wenwu*, 1981, no. 12, pp. 77–81, and in Howard Rogers and Sherman E. Lee, *Masterworks of Ming and Qing Painting from the Forbidden City* (Lansdale, Pa.: International Arts Council, 1988), p. 160.

12. Kenneth J. DeWoskin, *A Song for One or Two: Music and the Concept of Art in Early China* (Ann Arbor: Center for Chinese Studies, University of Michigan, 1982), p. 151. The nature of the relationship between art and politics during the Southern Dynasties period applies closely to their relationship in Cheng's time, and my discussion is adopted largely from DeWoskin's comments.

13. Theodore de Bary et al., *The Unfolding of Neo-Confucianism*, Studies in Oriental Studies (New York: Columbia University Press, 1970), pp. 16–18; John A. Hay "Huang Kung-wang" (Ph.D. diss., Princeton University, 1978), pp. 284–85.

14. Dong Qichang, "Huashuo," quoted in Osvald Siren, *Chinese Painting: Leading Masters and Principles* (London: Percy Lund, Humpheries and Co., 1958), 5:15; Chou Ju-hsi, "In Quest of the Primordial Line: The Genesis and Content of Tao-chi's 'Hua-yu-lu'" (Ph.D. diss., Princeton University, 1970); Dong Qichang, quoted in Wai-kam Ho, "Tung Ch'i-ch'ang's New Orthodoxy and the Southern School Theory," in *Artists and Traditions*, ed. Christian F. Murk (Princeton, N.J.: Princeton University Press, 1976), pp. 122–23; Ni Zan, trans. by Norbert Guterman, in François Fourcade, *Art Treasures of the Peking Museum* (New York: Harry N. Abrams, 1965), p. 40.

15. May Anna Quan Pang, "Wang Yuan-ch'i and Formal Construction in Chinese Landscape Painting" (Ph.D. diss., University of California, Berkeley, 1976), pp. 140–47.

Further Reading

Barnhart, Richard M. *Peach Blossom Spring: Gardens and Flowers in Chinese Paintings*. New York: Metropolitan Museum of Art, 1983.

A sensitive presentation of traditional nature symbolism as it appears in both painting and poetry.

Bush, Susan, and Christian Murk, eds. *Theories of the Arts in China*. Princeton, N.J.: Princeton University Press, 1983.

A selection of recent studies by various leading scholars exploring the diverse aspects of Chinese art theory.

de Bary, Theodore, ed. *The Unfolding of Neo-Confucianism*. Studies in Oriental Studies. New York: Columbia University Press, 1970.

An important anthology of scholarship that clarifies the nature of Neo-Confucianism's role in the Chinese mind from the late Song dynasty onward.

Goepper, Roger. *The Essence of Chinese Painting*. Boston: Boston Book and Art Shop, 1963.

A classic, illuminating summation of Chinese aesthetics, which still inspires all students of Chinese art history.

Li, Chu-tsing, and James C. Y. Watt, eds. *The Chinese Scholar's Studio: Artistic Life in the Late Ming Period*. New York: Asia Society Galleries in association with Thames and Hudson, 1987.

An exhibition catalogue that presents an evocative reconstruction of the life of Chinese aesthetes and the milieu and ambience in which they immersed themselves to engage in aesthetic dialogue and to create art.

Silbergeld, Jerome. "Chinese Concepts of Old Age and Their Role in Chinese Painting, Painting Theory, and Criticism." *Art Journal* 46, no. 2 (1987): 103–14.

An interesting study on the major but heretofore unexplored subject of the symbolism of immortality in Chinese art.

A Scholar's Garden in Ming China: Dream and Reality

Jan Stuart

Wandering in the Garden, Waking from a Dream (Youyuan jingmeng), a popular opera based on the Ming dynasty drama *The Peony Pavilion* (Mudan ting), alludes to a compelling aspect of Chinese gardens. The title would be even more descriptive if it were "Wandering in a Garden, *Entering* a Dream," because scholars' gardens of the Ming dynasty (1368–1644) were contrived to foster dreams. The garden was the setting in which a scholar tried to achieve ultimate moral perfection, a central goal in the syncretic blend of Buddhist, Confucian and Daoist thought popular during the Ming dynasty. Though designed to encourage the quest for transcendence, Ming gardens were at the same time an earthly paradise for those who realized the dream of self-cultivation, those sometimes called "earthly immortals" (*dixian*) in Daoist parlance.

In spite of the highly structured character of Chinese gardens and their pervasive use of imagery, Westerners have persistently perceived them as "naturalistic." Father Attiret, for example, an early missionary to China, reported in Paris in 1749 that Chinese gardens were "Works of Nature."[1] He

was mistaken. Nature *and* artifice have always comfortably comingled in Chinese gardens, and artifice, in fact, predominates. This detail of Yi Yuan (Pleasure Garden) in Suzhou depicts the modern restoration of a garden built during the Ming dynasty and greatly expanded during the late 1800s (fig. 1). The visitor enters a courtyard through a round opening, which by avoiding the rectilinear shape of a doorway in a formal building, transports him to an extraordinary realm. The rocks inside were chosen for their bizarre shapes, while the greenery is very natural. The "ground cover" is terracotta tiles since the garden designer did not feel bound to mimic nature and found tile superior to grass or earth. Its surface is comfortable to walk upon and ideal for reflecting the shadow of rocks and trees on a moonlit night. Ming gardens like this one, reflecting the acme of garden design and serving as models for centuries to come, were dream visions.

The Ming Background

The Ming dynasty was less purely agrarian than earlier periods. A

Detail, *The Garden for Self-Enjoyment*. See figure 4.

money-based economy began to flourish, which in turn fostered urbanization and general prosperity, especially in cities south of the Yangtze River such as Suzhou. Suzhou's bustling economy attracted educated literati as well as nouveau riche, who imitated the scholars' lifestyle as much as possible. Since gardens had been an important accoutrement to scholarly life since at least the Six Dynasties (265–589), and as Suzhou had a gentle climate, plentiful water, and fame as a handicraft center, it was inevitable that the city experienced an unprecedented flurry of garden building. Ming editions of the *Suzhou Gazetteer* (*Suzhou fuzhi*), the official record of the region, boasted nearly three hundred gardens worthy enough to record by name.

Most Suzhou gardens were part of larger residential complexes of which only about one-third was devoted to the garden proper. Ming gardens were smaller than in earlier periods, and they were usually separated from the formal living quarters by a wall with a gate or were built off to the side. The garden design thus did not have to follow certain conventions, such as geomancy (*fengshui*), which dictated the placement of permanent residences and graves. The only absolute rule governing garden buildings according to *Yuan ye* (Forging a Garden), the first important treatise on garden design, was that they take advantage of the scenery, as does this open-air kiosk in Zhuozheng Yuan (Garden of the Artless Official; fig. 2). The kiosk, perhaps not original to the famous Suzhou garden built in 1513, nonetheless exemplifies the tradition of siting a building near water, rocks, and attractive trees or plants. *Yuan ye* was written by Ji Cheng (born 1582) from Suzhou in the late Ming dynasty, about 1634. It provides some of the most important evidence for understanding Ming gardens.

The Ego and the Garden

The Chinese garden was a world unto itself. As the modern scholar Wing-tsit Chan succinctly describes:

The garden is a place where [man] . . . reveals his nature, the base as well as the noble. In short, man asserts himself in the garden, and turns it into an area for the expansion of his ego.[2]

Although this description is timeless, it applies particularly well to Ming and later gardens. The bond between personal ego and the garden was so strong that many scholars used the name of their garden or a site in it as a personal sobriquet. One example is Wang Xianchen (*jinshi* degree, 1493), builder of the Garden of the Artless Official, who called himself Huaiyu (Rain in the Pagoda Tree [*Sophora japonica*]) after his favorite garden pavilion. The custom of choosing a personal name related to one's garden dates back at least to the time of the famous poet and recluse Tao Qian (365–427), who wrote a thinly veiled autobiography in which he called himself Master Five Willows after his garden.

The connection between a man's identity and his garden led to the Ming view that garden design was, like painting and poetry, an expression of the self. According to *Yuan ye* a proprietor should be personally responsible for nine-tenths of his garden's design. Professional designer-craftsmen

Base and Noble Dreams

Wing-tsit Chan highlights a fundamental principle in explaining that the garden is a place to reveal both "base" and "noble" characteristics. A person was supposed to reveal his true nature in the garden setting, where he could be the uninhibited self of dreams rather than the follower of formal social etiquette. The "base" that Wing-tsit Chan refers to includes frivolous garden recreations and amusements as well as passion. Gardens were often, in fact, the setting for love in Chinese literature and painting.

Wandering in the Garden, Waking from a Dream, which recounts a story of love fulfilled through a dream in a garden, offers a prime example. A scholar's daughter falls asleep in the garden on a hot spring day and dreams of a passionate tryst with a young gentleman. Awake, she languishes for her dream-lover until she falls ill and dies. The story concludes with her return to life after a real-life counterpart of her dream-lover falls in love with her portrait, thus causing the judge of the underworld to bring her back to life.

The story draws attention to the convention of setting amorous scenes in a garden. The privacy of a walled garden, the allure of blooming flowers, which since ancient times were often used as emblems for female beauty, and perhaps even the rocks—some of which have phallic shapes—are ideally suited to flame love and passion. But the opera also illuminates a telling point about the Ming attitude toward dreams. The maiden completely satisfies her passion in a dream, suggesting a function of dreams that has a corollary in Daoist and Buddhist

Figure 1. Detail, Pleasure Garden (Yi Yuan), Suzhou, 1985. The garden was built during the Ming dynasty and greatly expanded in the Guangxu reign (1875–1909) of the Qing dynasty.

like Ji Cheng were theoretically to be used only to solve technical problems and coordinate the actual building. The existence of Ji Cheng's manual, however, strongly suggests that while personal expression was a garden proprietor's goal, there were enough standard conventions to warrant writing a book about them.

medical literature of the period. Dreams were interpreted as vital links between the mind and body and deemed to have the power to affect the reality of a dreamer's life.[3] Although the dream in this opera is the product of sleep, Ming culture was equally concerned with dreams that were conscious longings for something more "noble."

Sleep researcher David Foulkes has posited that dreams "portray moral standards different from those that control, at least overtly, waking behavior."[4] While Western psychologists tend to believe that a dreamer wants to escape from social mores and act without restraint, especially in regard to sexual behavior, Ming accounts describe an entirely different kind of escape. The Ming garden occupant dreamed of escaping the vexations that held him back from perfecting himself according to the Confucian, Daoist, and Buddhist mores that controlled his waking behavior.

A scholar's garden was built as a moral cosmos where the scholar could dream of becoming a true man (*zhenren*) and an immortal (*xian*), which, although both originally Daoist terms, by Ming times had become

Figure 2. Garden of the Artless Official, Suzhou, originally built in 1513, during the Ming dynasty.

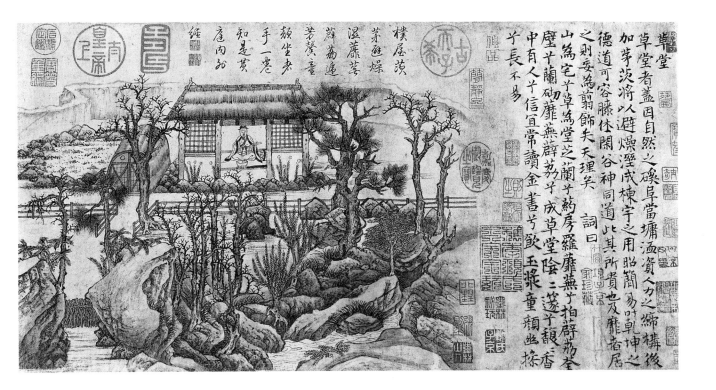

草堂

草堂者蓋因自然之磧阜當塗溢資人力之繕構後

加茅茨將以避燥濕成棟宇之用此其所貴也及靡者居

德道可容藤休閑谷神同道易叶乾坤之

之則妄為翦飾失天理矣

山為宅兮草為堂芝蘭兮藥房羅薦薇兮指辟荔兮

塵兮蘭砌靡燕莪辟荔兮成草堂陰二篆兮馥香

中有人兮信宜常讀兮書兮飲玉漿童顏兮

兮長不多

詞曰

Figure 3. Detail, Song dynasty copy after Lu Hong, *Ten Views of a Thatched Hut*, 8th century, Tang dynasty. Handscroll, ink on paper, 11¹/₂ × 234 in. The National Palace Museum, Taiwan, Republic of China

accepted as descriptions of a lofty man. In fact, the majority of gardens were made after a scholar retired from government service, a standard occupation for most scholars, who were influenced by Confucianism to believe it was noble to serve the state. By the mid-Ming dynasty, however, the court was corrupt and a government servant who could not be bribed had little chance of remaining unscathed. He could protect his moral integrity only by invoking the principle of Confucian eremitism and retiring early as a gesture of protest. The honest scholar then withdrew into semiseclusion inside his walled garden.

The Dream of Transcendence

The transcendence that a retired scholar sought was not an epochal event like the Western idea of becoming a saint after death but rather involved the perfection of one's inner energies and moral self in a process of continuous regeneration. In the Chinese view a person could move back and forth between the state of immortality and normal life. The morally pure environment of a garden could, accordingly, cause a proprietor "to find . . . relaxation . . . [and] happiness; [and] know how to enjoy life, which is to become an Immortal."[5] These are the words of Ji Cheng.

The quest for immortality is basic to Chinese culture, and its connection with gardens dates at least to the Han dynasty (206 B.C.–A.D. 220), when Emperor Wu (reigned 140–87 B.C.) designed three islands in a garden pond to resemble the home of the immortals, who reputedly lived on islands in the great sea. Wu hoped to tempt the sylphs to alight in the imperial garden by giving them an acceptable substitute for their domicile, thus establishing a precedent that gardens could effectively substitute for less mundane realms of existence.

A deep association between dreams and immortality was also a common cultural premise. By the late Tang dynasty (618–907) the dream journey to the paradise of the immortals was a well-established literary theme. One of the most eloquent examples dates to the tenth century, just after the fall of the Tang. Guanxiu, a Buddhist monk and poet, wrote four poems collectively entitled *Dream of a Journey to the Land of the Immortals* (Mengyou xian), which blended Daoist and Buddhist lore. Many of the images Guanxiu chose in his writing—to quote from the scholar Edward Schafer—"saw impressed on the gardens of this world the image of the deathless garden of the spirit."[6] Intimately aware of these historical precedents, Ming scholars believed that a good design could transform their gardens into a paradise of the immortals.

Like literature, painting recorded the early association between gardens and immortality. One of the earliest paintings to depict a garden was Lu Hong's (active 713–741) *Ten Views of a Thatched Hut*, which survives in a Song dynasty (960–1279) copy now in the Palace Museum, Taiwan, but which was widely circulated among the Suzhou literati during the sixteenth century. Lu Hong illustrated his reclusive mountain retreat in ten scenes, for each of which he wrote an accompanying poem. The first scene in the painting shows his studio and is accompanied by a poem which con-

cludes by explaining that there he read the "golden books" of religious Daoism and partook of a "jade sauce" that was an elixir of immortality (fig. 3). Another site in Lu Hong's garden was called "Steps to Await the Immortals."

Herb plots that featured plants known for life-prolonging powers were also typical garden sites. Ming proprietors seriously followed the custom of establishing herb plots, which had ancient antecedents. One of the Four Masters of Ming Painting, Qiu Ying (1494–1552), illustrates both the Ming fascination with herb plots and the historical precedent in his painting *The Garden for Self-Enjoyment*, which is an imaginary reconstruction of Sima Guang's (1019–1086) garden but incorporates many Ming stylistic features (fig. 4). In the large herb plot Qiu Ying depicts a giant frond of the fungus of immortality (*lingzhi*), among other medicinal plants.

Scale

Ming gardens were marked by an abandon and distortion of the logical rules of time and space, thereby creating a dreamlike quality. In fact, gardens were built without any unifying scale; instead, each element was independent. The viewer had constantly to reinterpret the garden along an expanding and contracting continuum. Rocks, for example, were supposed to be viewed as if they were mountains. The visitor might observe miniature landscapes in table-size pots while leisurely resting in a full-size pavilion. Thus a few acres could encompass a grand cosmic vision. As Ji Cheng explained, "A smaller layout roughly formed may be sufficient to evoke a total view."

The Neo-Confucian principle of Extension of Knowledge in the Investigation of Things was a paradigm for Ji Cheng's assessment. It taught that learning based on observation of things at hand such as garden elements could be applied to broad categories of similar objects to reveal the inner patterns of cosmic existence. Ming garden designers believed that the vastness of the universe could be made intelligible if one could "see the small in the large, see the large in the small, see the real in the illusory and the illusory in the real," which is how Shen Fu characterized his garden in *Six Chapters of a Floating Life* (Fusheng liuji, ca. 1809). Shen Fu, a native of Suzhou who lived into the early nineteenth century, carried on the tradition of Ming garden style. He elaborated when he described his youth in the garden:

I used to crouch down by the hollows and protrusions of the mud wall or among the tangled grasses . . . so that I was on the same level as the flower beds. Then I would compose myself and look closely, until the clumps of grass became a forest, the ants and other insects became wild beasts, the clods and pebbles which jutted up were hills, and those which sank down were valleys. My spirit roamed freely in this world and I felt completely at ease.[7]

Shen Fu's exposition is one of the most eloquent on the telescoping scale that ruled the garden world, but Chinese literature abounds with similar examples.

From Small to Large: *Penjing* to *Jiashan*

Ming paintings also illustrate the sliding scale of garden design. Qiu Ying's *Pleasure in a Wooded Pavilion* depicts a low stone table on which two *penjing* (tray landscapes) are set (fig. 5). A warm brown-colored pot (perhaps of Yixing clay) contains a miniature pine tree, which, because of its association with longevity, was often selected for *penjing*. A larger pot contains a stone —which is a "miniature" mountain— the base of which is fringed by blades of calamus sweet flag (*Acorus gramineus soland*). Sweet flag was frequently cultivated as an ingredient for the elixir of immortality.

In this painting Qiu Ying reproduces the visual punning that a visitor to the real garden would have experienced. The diminutive pine tree on the table echoes a full-size one on the opposite shore of the lake, and the potted stone with its tiny holes plays against the large boulder from Lake Tai at the right of the pavilion, itself also a miniature mountain, albeit on a larger scale. Sword-blade leaves of cymbidium orchids at its base parallel the effect of the sweet flag in the tray landscape, reinforcing the visual connection. With his artist's brush Qiu Ying indicated the interplay of scale that all garden visitors would have been aware of even if they could not see it as clearly. Qiu Ying painted real mountains as a backdrop, for all the rock elements inside the garden alluded to these majestic peaks. But in actuality Suzhou had no major mountains, and Tiger Hill would have been visible only from a second-story building. Precisely to take advantage of the

Figure 4. Detail, Qiu Ying, *The Garden for Self-Enjoyment*, ca. 1547, Ming dynasty. Handscroll, ink and color on silk, 10⁷/8 × 148⁵/8 in. The Cleveland Museum of Art, John L. Severance Fund

interplay between the macrocosmic world and the microcosm of the garden, most proprietors built one two-story structure from which they could see over the garden walls.

Another favorite way to furnish a garden with mountain images was to use natural slabs of marble with gray and black striations that look like paintings of mountainscapes. During the Ming dynasty and later, inset marble tablets served as table tops, chair seats, and back slats. Pieces of marble were also framed as room-size screens, table screens, and wall hangings. In *Man Cleaning His Ear* the top of the scholar's writing table is a large piece of marble; the mountain forms suggested by the dark striations in the stone are echoed by the porcelain brushrest that is shaped like three conical peaks (fig. 6). At the back of the room the large painted landscape is yet another example of "indoor" and "garden-scale" mountain imagery.

Westerners who learned of this type of marble from the Chinese called it "dream stone" and "journey stone," terms that, although not used by the Chinese, suggest the attitude a Chinese

scholar had when he used this marble in his garden. For him, the marble inspired imaginary journeys through tall mountains. The Chinese sometimes poetically called the marble "peach blossom stone," undoubtedly in reference not to a flower shape but to Tao Qian's literary masterpiece "Record of the Peach Blossom Spring" (Taohuayuan ji, ca. 397–405), a story of a dreamlike journey to a utopia that a fisherman discovered after stepping through a mountain cave.

The elements in a Chinese garden that are most renowned for the dream-like innuendo of distorting scale are the *jiashan*, or imitation mountains. Whether a *jiashan* was made from a solitary boulder, a group of stones, or packed earth, viewers took the attitude that it was coequal with a real mountain. This attitude followed the tradition of Zong Bing (375–443), a famous Buddhist and Daoist adept who was one of the first to write about the irrelevance of spatial boundaries in "Preface to Landscape Painting" (Hua shanshui xu, ca. 433–43). When Zong Bing became too infirm to roam in the mountains as was his wont, he realized that landscape paintings offered a spirit journey that was a perfect substitute for hiking. According to Zong, a vertical stroke of three inches equaled thousands of feet and the towering peak of Mount Kunlun, a haunt of the immortals, was encompassed in a square inch. Zong Bing called his spiritual journeys *woyou* (traveling while lying down, or dream journeys). It is not coincidental that twelve hundred years later Ji Cheng used the same term to describe strolling in a garden.

Attitudes toward Nature and Artifice

Yuan ye elucidated the Ming scholar's attitude toward nature. Ji Cheng noted that ideally a garden site should have "natural attractions," such as old trees, but it was definitely expected that the site would be altered to correspond with the proprietor's preconceived garden plan. For example, Ji Cheng said:

If there are trees which have stood for many years that would get in the way of the eaves or walls of your building . . . lop off a few branches to avoid the roof.

He also said:

For every ten parts of land, three should be made into a pond . . . preferably made by dredging out an existing stream. Of the remaining seven-tenths, four should be built up with earth . . . and be planted with bamboo in a harmonious way.[8]

The Ming concept of what was "natural" differs from the modern. According to Ji Cheng, "If you have the real to make the imitation, then when you make the imitation it will become real." Thus someone familiar with actual mountains could treat the assemblages of rocks in a garden as if they were real mountains. A more extreme blurring between nature and artifice was Ji Cheng's comment made without irony: "The whole area [of this garden], a natural work of art, will resemble Yinghu, the land of the Immortals"[9] (Yinghu is one of the three mythical islands that are the home of the immortals). To judge from Ming paintings of the islands, they were magically contorted towers of rock that could not be called natural, yet Ji Cheng was apparently unaware of any cognitive dissonance in his statement.

The Ming understanding of what was natural, artificial, or magical was fluid. An attractive garden island, whether man-made or not, could inspire Ji Cheng to exclaim "A natural work of art!" while symbolizing, at the same time, the magical Yinghu. An example of the island effect that Ji Cheng spoke of was captured by the famous Suzhou literatus and painter Shen Zhou (1427–1509) in *Studio in a Bamboo Grove* (fig. 7). The painting depicts an island with a studio, pavilion, and two-story belvedere on it. A plank bridge connects the island to the shore, where there is a garden kiosk. Although the painting makes the island look natural, it was probably fashioned out of soil dredged from making the pond in which it sits. What look like precipitous foothills in the painting were probably only *jiashan*.

Shen Zhou was a principled, retiring man who believed in the Confucian ideal that sages led a simple life. Some of his painting inscriptions reveal exactly how he used his garden as a setting for inner cultivation. On *Night Vigil*, which depicts a slightly different view of the same garden portrayed in *Studio in a Bamboo Grove*, Shen wrote that he spent many hours in his garden "cleansing the mind, waiting through the long watches by the light of a candle [which] becomes the basis of an inner peace and of an understanding of things."[10]

Shen Zhou emphasized the pure and simple life in the vein of Confucian eremitism. Yet because of the common association between loftiness and status as a *xian*, the island in his garden imitated the immortals' Yinghu. Still, it represented at the same time the achievement of transcendence by the cleansing of the mind and served as an emblem for reaching moral perfection.

The Principle of Yin and Yang

As most Suzhou gardens unfolded scene by scene instead of offering a panoramic expanse, they are called "strolling gardens" or, as the modern garden historian Chen Congzhou says, "in-motion" gardens. A garden was divided into sections by walls, roofed corridors (which often had a solid wall on one side and open latticework on the other), wattle fences, and trellis walls covered with plants. Imitation mountains also partitioned the space. The Qiu Ying attribution *The Garden of the Daily Scripture Lesson* offers an aerial view of a typical Ming garden that was compartmentalized into discrete courtyards (fig. 8). Because only one section at a time was therefore visible, it was impossible to predict what the garden was like or how large it was. This division of space was an

effective way to make small properties seem larger than they were. Although the concept of "in-motion" was an essential feature in Suzhou gardens, the Chinese predilection to pair opposite qualities made a sense of "repose" equally important.

The concept of paired opposites derived from the ancient explanation of the cyclical interaction of yin and yang, bipolar opposites, as the basis of creation, itself an ongoing process. Expressions of this dualism occur in many art forms, including gardens. A garden's ability simultaneously to suggest the action of journeying to paradise and the tranquillity of being there was a perfect articulation of yin and yang.

The garden visitor had to move through a garden physically in order to see it all. Decoratively paved pathways and beguilingly shaped doorways helped draw the visitor from one area to the next by emphasizing the dynamic sequence of sites to be visited—courtyards, buildings, watery spots, rock formations, and plants.

The Nine Elders of the Mountain of Fragrance, attributed to the Ming artist Xie Huan (active 1426–1452), depicts the appeal that paths pebbled with river-smoothed stones exerted to tempt a visitor forward (fig. 9). The tactile quality of slightly uneven stones and their warm, lustrous colors summoned the visitors to follow them. The subject of this painting is a literary gathering that occurred in 845, but Xie Huan painted a garden of his own period.

Although gardens were laid out to make the visitor feel as if he were journeying through one, many features were also designed to tempt the visitor

to sit and rest. Elegant buildings, often partially open, that offered sensational views were placed throughout the garden. The most common buildings were small pavilions called *ting*, which, although written differently, sounds like the word that means "to stop" (*ting*). Ji Cheng noted this pun in *Yuan ye*.

From the vantage point of a pavilion, the visitor experienced "motion in repose." While seated, a scholar could contemplate scudding clouds and rippling water or take an imaginary mountainous journey by gazing at the imitation mountains in the garden. The holes that pierced the boulders were read as caves, and the pitted, knobby texture and sharp turns of the stone's silhouette became precipitous paths. Xie Huan painted a servant in the act of placing stools inside a *ting*, a detail nicely pointing out how the scholar in the garden was expected to rest in the *ting* while gazing at the nearby Lake Tai rock-mountain.

To parallel "motion in repose," the garden also had to cultivate the quality of "repose in motion." The same rocks that stimulated fantasies of active mountain climbing took on a different role when viewed by a strolling visitor. From this frame of reference they were steadfast monuments likened to China's great peaks. Likewise the tiny ripples in a garden pond that might seem like waves to the contemplative viewer were insignificant to the moving visitor. To him the water seemed smooth and motionless like a mirror, a common literary cliché in garden descriptions.

Another typical expression of the paradox of motion and repose was the peculiar manner of standing solitary boulders from Lake Tai on their narrow end to represent a mountain peak. Though the monolith seemed about to overturn at any moment, a large piece of the rock was buried underground to act as an anchor. The sensation of potential motion created by this unbalanced arrangement was a valued allusion to yin and yang; the rock that should be stable (repose) was on the verge of tumbling over (motion).

Magical Openings: Garden Caves

The doorways in the fences and walls that divided a strolling garden into sections were an important aspect of the dream ethos. Some of the openings were fanciful shapes—circles, leaves, gourds, or jars—but even a standard rectangular opening that provided a glimpse from one courtyard into the next was special. Ji Cheng hinted at the subliminal power of doorways whose purpose, he said, was to allow one to look "secretly . . . through them into different worlds, as if in a magic flask"—a reference to the realm of the immortals.

Many of the doorways and windows in garden walls were round and, like the openings in the imitation mountains, suggested a cave. In Daoist tradition the entrance to paradise was a cave. Another related cultural association held that caves led to an earthly utopia, as in Tao Qian's "Peach Blossom Spring."

Round passages are commonly referred to as "moon gates," but the term did not become popular until after the Ming dynasty. The chapter devoted to windows and gates in *Yuan*

Figure 6. Artist unknown, *Man Cleaning His Ear*, Ming dynasty. Handscroll, ink and color on silk, 12¹/₄ × 16¹/₂ in. Freer Gallery of Art, 11.486

ye shows a round window with the caption: "moon window style; if large, it can be used as a passageway." This is one of the earliest descriptions of a full-size doorway as moon shaped (see also the round doorway visible in fig. 1). Originally a round doorway was referred to as a "cave to pass through" (*yue dong*) or a "gate to pass through" (*yue men*). In Chinese the words "to pass through" and "moon" sound alike although written with different characters, and therefore the picturesque term "moon gate" gradually surpassed the popularity of the original term. But regardless of the

nomenclature, it was standard to interpret a round doorway as a symbolic entrance to a cave.

As the scholar Kiyohiko Munakata has observed, some garden architecture was also intentionally used to reflect cave imagery:

The many corridors or hallways provide dark passages that suddenly open, often through a cave-gate, to bright new worlds. These dimly lighted areas of transition have an effect of giving the visitor the illusion of walking through mysterious passages inside caves.[11]

The Ming garden suggesting areas

linked together by caves reflected the Daoist concept that the earth was connected to the immortals' paradise by a series of cave passages.

Rocks and Water

Rocks were clearly essential in gardens. The scholar John Hay aptly referred to them as "kernels of energy, bones of earth" in a book by that title written to explain the Chinese attitude toward stones and their appearance in art. Water was another basic garden ingredient and, as the antithesis of stone, created a balance of yin and yang. Indeed a cojoining of rocks and water imbued the garden with the metaphoric meaning as an extended landscape or microcosm since the Chinese word for "landscape" (*shanshui*) literally means "mountains and waters."

Confucius alluded in book 6 of the *Analects* to the import of rocks and water: "The wise [*zhi*] man delights in water, the humane [*ren*] man delights in the mountains." In that vein a garden rock and pond were symbols that encouraged a garden proprietor to seek self-perfection through communion with nature. The word *zhi* encompasses both knowledge and wisdom, and therefore a man of *zhi* is a sage. *Ren* means goodness, benevolence, and humaneness, qualities requisite for self-perfection. Confucius also said men of *ren* live long, a testament to their harmony with nature.

In the world of Ming thought, where Confucian, Daoist, and Buddhist notions constantly intermingled, a Confucian scholar who delighted in his garden's imitation mountains and pond was aspiring to be "good" and "wise" in the sense of Confucius. Simultaneously the extended life span of the sage and humane man intersected with the Daoist notion of the immortals. The garden was therefore both moral cosmos and the pleasure grounds of the immortals.

The Garden as a Whole

Having considered some of the component parts of Ming gardens, we can now turn to an overview. Although some gardens founded during the Ming dynasty are extant in modern Suzhou, they have been so altered that it is better to look at Ming paintings to understand the period. One painting

that provides an overview of a garden is *The Garden of the Daily Scripture Lesson,* attributed to Qiu Ying but which is more likely by an anonymous follower (see fig. 8). The garden was named after a Buddhist practice of studying a lesson a day toward the goal of enlightenment; it is a scholar's garden, however, not part of a monastery. The term "daily lesson" (*qingke*), in fact, occurs in several Ming paintings of gardens, for during that period it took on the broader meaning of any personal search for self-cultivation.

It is clear from a detail taken from the lower right that *The Garden of the Daily Scripture Lesson* depicts a scholar's private garden (see fig. 8a). A young servant is pictured washing his master's ink stone in the garden pond. As a trickle of ink turns the water jet black, the viewer is reminded of the legend of the calligraphy sage Wang Xizhi (ca. A.D. 307–ca. 365), who reputedly practiced his art so diligently that the pond in which he cleaned his ink stone and brushes turned black. This comparison elevated the proprietor of the garden depicted in the painting to a par with the great scholars of the past, a favorite Chinese manner of ennoblement.

The painting provides an architectural tour of a garden as well as showing how different components relate to each other. It echoes the concerns we expect to find in a Ming garden. Note, for example, the pot of calamus sweet

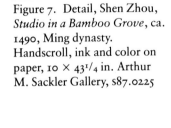

Figure 7. Detail, Shen Zhou, *Studio in a Bamboo Grove*, ca. 1490, Ming dynasty. Handscroll, ink and color on paper, 10 × 43¹/₄ in. Arthur M. Sackler Gallery, s87.0225

Figure 8. Attributed to Qiu Ying, *The Garden of the Daily Scripture Lesson*, 16th or 17th century, Ming dynasty. Hanging scroll, ink and color on silk, 32¼ × 41½ in. The National Palace Museum, Taiwan, Republic of China

Figure 8a. Detail

flag on a table in the lower right corner and two more pots of it on a table in midground. The animal guests—a spotted deer and two cranes, both symbols of immortality—corroborate the garden's association with a quest for immortality. Even the detail of a servant setting up a game of *weiqi*, or chess, although a standard leisure activity, also alludes to immortality since it is a game favored by the immortals (see fig. 8b).

The most interesting architectural component is the pavilion in the lower right corner that is made from four trees whose branches were intertwined into a roof. In the mistaken spirit of Father Attiret, Westerners continue to believe that Chinese gardens never had clipped trees, topiaries, or espaliers, but many paintings reveal exactly these artifices, although not so frequently or in such elaborate detail as in formal European gardens. The difference between Western and Chinese gardens is much more than one being more naturalistic; rather, it is that Chinese gardens are fundamentally thought-pictures (to borrow a term from David Foulkes) or dreams of personal transcendence.

Ming Commentary on Dreams and Gardens

Ming writings add credence to the understanding of the Ming garden as a dream world, for the word "dream" (*meng*), in fact, often occurs in Ming scholars' descriptions and poems about gardens. The Ming scholar-official and garden builder Chi Biaojia (1602–1645) provides an example of how dreams could be the very inspiration for a garden. He wrote in *Yushanju* (Remarks on Yushan Garden, ca. 1635) that he relied on dreams for the layout of his garden, although it is also said that the contemporaneous garden designer Zhang Lian was of much help to him.

Figure 8b. Detail

Figure 9. Attributed to Xie Huan, *The Nine Elders of the Mountain of Fragrance*, 15th century, Ming dynasty. Handscroll, ink and color on silk, 11 5/8 × 57 3/4 in. Intended gift to The Cleveland Museum of Art, Mr. and Mrs. A. Dean Perry

Chi Biaojia makes some standard observations about his garden: where it was too empty he added something, but where it was full he removed things; where it was crowded he thinned it out, and where it was sparse he made clusters. Chi Biaojia explains that originally he did not have a clear plan for his garden, but then images came to him in dreams. As he walked through the garden he began to visualize pavilions and studios dotting the land, and he saw images in dreams that opened new vistas.[12] Chi never specified if his visions were the product of sleep or daydreams, but they were powerful enough to determine the final layout of his property.

Dreams apparently could both shape a Ming property and provide its essential meaning. The major artist Wen Zhengming (1470–1559) illustrated in an album of poetry and painting that he made for his friend Wang Xianchen how the Garden of the Artless Official was tied to dreams. Using the paradisal palette of blue and green mineral colors and ink, Wen Zhengming painted thirty-one sites in the garden in an album dated 1533.

The word "dream" occurs several times in the poetry that Wen wrote in the album. One example is the second leaf, which depicts the site known as "Dreaming of Retirement Belvedere" (Mengyin lou; fig. 10). Wen Zhengming's preface and poem read:

"Dreaming of Retirement Belvedere" is above Canglang Pond. . . . Master [Wang Xianchen] went to Jiuli Lake [in Fujian Province—famous for a story of nine boys who became immortals there] and sought divine help in his dream for retirement and obtained it. . . .
Forests and springs enter dreams of boundless longing,
When a tall belvedere arises withdraw into seclusion. . . .
From within the pillow [world] I've awakened to the illusion of officialdom. . . .
I turn my head toward where the imperial capital once was,
Leaning on a balustrade I see only the hoary mountains at sunset.

The poem explains that Wang Xianchen built his garden from a dream or longing to retire from government service. Staunchly honest, he had encountered numerous hardships because he could not be bribed, and so, in the spirit of Confucian eremitism, he retired rather than give his services to a corrupt emperor.

The dream mentioned is an allusion to the Tang-dynasty story "The World within a Pillow" (Zhenzhong ji), which characterized the vanity of official-dom. It relates the adventures of a commoner who longs to become an official and shares his aspiration with a fellow traveler, a Daoist adept, in an inn. The Daoist lends the commoner his pillow, and, once asleep, the commoner finds it has opened into a magic world where he is an official. Here he must endure slanderous attacks for trying to be honest, and when he awakes he realizes that a good man is better off not entering officialdom.

This dream is an analogue for Wang Xianchen's real-life experiences, and certain details, such as the postings to Shenxi and Guangdong, match the specifics of Wang Xianchen's career. This coincidence was not lost on Wen Zhengming.

The painting reinforces the mood of the poem. The two-story garden building is far removed from the bustle of the world, and its hidden occupant could gaze no farther than the colored mountains that blocked the horizon toward the capital. At the base of the belvedere a grove of flowering peach trees alludes to Tao Qian's "Peach Blossom Spring"—yet another signal that Wang Xianchen's garden was a dreamland utopia in which he could reach moral perfection.

Dream Visions

Ming scholars dreamed of transcendence. In their quest they developed a special way of life in which the bound-

Figure 10. Wen Zhengming, *Dreaming of Retirement Belvedere*. Leaf from the album *The Garden of the Artless Official*, dated 1533. Ink and color on silk, app. 10 × 12 in. Collection unknown

aries between the inner and outer world became blurred, exemplified in their naming themselves after their gardens. For them the distinction between reality and dreams was diminished, and even Sigmund Freud admitted the value of such a perception. "Dreams do not consist," he wrote, "solely of illusion. If for instance, one is afraid of robbers in a dream, the robbers, it is true, are imaginary—but the fear is real."[13]

In the same light, the Ming scholar's garden that inspired a dream journey toward the goal of transcendence—of mingling with Daoist immortals and attaining moral perfection as a Confucian hermit—may not have enabled a garden dweller to ride a crane to para-

dise or to avoid all moral crises, but it did provide the means for a man to believe he could perfect his moral self.

Notes

1. For more about Father Attiret, see Maggie Keswick, *The Chinese Garden* (New York: Rizzoli International, 1978), pp. 9–11.

2. Wing-tsit Chan, "Man and Nature in the Chinese Garden," in *Chinese Houses and Gardens*, ed. Henry Inn, 2d ed. (New York: Hastings House, 1950), p. 30. I learned of this statement in the excellent article by Kiyohiko Munakata, "Mysterious Heavens and Chinese Classical Gardens," *Res* 15 (Spring 1988): 61.

3. See Carolyn T. Brown, ed., *Psycho-Sinology: The Universe of Dreams in Chinese Culture* (Washington, D.C.: Asia Program, Woodrow Wilson International Center, 1987), esp. the essays by Robert Hegel, "Heavens and Hells in Chinese Fictional Dreams," pp. 1–10, and Michel Strickmann, "Dreamwork of Psycho-Sinologists, Doctors, Taoists, Monks," pp. 25–46.

4. David Foulkes, *A Grammar of Dreams* (New York: Basic Books, 1978), pp. 31–32. I was introduced to this book through Brown, *Psycho-Sinology*.

5. Ji Cheng, *The Craft of Gardens*, trans. Alison Hardie (New Haven, Conn.: Yale University Press, 1988), p. 53. Subsequent references are to Hardie's translation unless otherwise noted. Citation by page will only be given for long quotations.

6. Edward H. Schafer, "Mineral Imagery in the Paradise Poems of Kuan-hsui [Guanxiu]," *Asia Major*, n.s. 10, pt. 1 (1963): 83. I would like to thank Stephen Allee for referring this article to me.

7. Shen Fu, *Fusheng liuji*, trans. by Andrew Plaks, in *Archetype and Allegory in the Dream of the Red Chamber* (Princeton, N.J.: Princeton University Press, 1976), p. 164.

8. Ji Cheng, *Craft of Gardens*, pp. 45–46, 49.

9. Ibid., p. 65.

10. Shen Zhou, quoted in Richard Edwards, *The Field of Stones* (Washington, D.C.: Freer Gallery of Art, 1962), p. 57.

11. Munakata, "Mysterious Heavens and Chinese Classical Gardens," p. 75.

12. Chi Biaojia, "Yushanju," in *Zhongguo lidai mingyuan ji xuanju*, ed. Chen Zhi et al. (Anhui: Kexue Zhimu Chubanshe, 1983), p. 260.

13. Sigmund Freud, *The Interpretation of Dreams*, trans. James Strachey (New York: Avon Books, 1965), p. 106, cited by Wendy D. O'Flaherty, *Dreams, Illusions and Other Realities* (Chicago: University of Chicago Press, 1984), p. 45.

Further Reading

Bauer, Wolfgang. *China and the Search for Happiness*. Translated by Michael Shaw. New York: Seabury Press, 1976.

A detailed study with extensive references to original Chinese sources that defines the development and continuity of utopian thought in China from 1500 B.C. to the twentieth century.

Chen Congzhou. *Shuo yuan/On Chinese Gardens*. Bilingual ed. Translated by Chen Xiongshan et al. Shanghai: Tongji University Press, 1984.

A discussion of the basic design principles used in Chinese gardens, including quotations from Ming dynasty authors.

Chen Zhi et al., eds. *Zhongguo lidai mingyuanji xuanju* (Selected and Annotated Records of Famous Gardens throughout China's History). Anhui: Kexue zhimu chubanshe, 1983.

A collection of fifty-five records of gardens written between the Tang and Qing dynasties.

Hay, John. *Kernels of Energy, Bones of Earth: The Rock in Chinese Art*. New York: China Institute in America, 1985.

An exhibition catalogue that discusses the significance of the rock in Chinese culture and introduces examples of paintings and three-dimensional art objects that celebrate the theme of rocks.

Ho, Wai-kam. "Late Ming Literati: Their Social and Cultural Ambience." In *The Chinese Scholar's Studio: Artistic Life in the Late Ming Period*, edited by Chu-tsing Li and James C. Y. Watt, pp. 23–36. New York: Asia Society Galleries in association with Thames and Hudson, 1987.

A discussion of the Jiajing (1522–66) and Wanli (1573–1620) eras of the Ming dynasty that focuses on the rich prefectural and county seat Jiaxing, south of Lake Tai, as a typical representation of the literati lifestyle.

Ji Cheng. *Yuan ye*. Translated by Alison Hardie as *The Craft of Gardens*. New Haven, Conn.: Yale University Press, 1988.

The earliest major treatise on garden design in China, combining practical advice about how to build a garden with discussions on philosophic meaning. Hardie's translation is the only complete English translation.

Kerby, Kate, ed. *An Old Chinese Garden*. Shanghai: Zhonghua Book Company, [ca. 1922].

A reproduction and translation (albeit rather outdated and problematic) of Wen Zhengming's 1533 album of *The Garden of the Artless Official*.

Keswick, Maggie. *The Chinese Garden*. New York: Rizzoli International, 1978.

A basic introduction with copious illustrations of Chinese gardens, including imperial and literati gardens and topics such as architecture, rocks and water, and plants.

Laing, Ellen. "Qiu Ying's Description of Sima Guang's Duluo Yuan and the View from the Chinese Garden." *Oriental Art* n.s. 33, no. 5 (Winter 1987–88): 375–80.

An examination of the sixteenth-century master Qiu Ying's handscroll of Sima Guang's eleventh-century garden that offers insights into the cultural significance of gardens, especially with reference to looking back to the past.

Munakata, Kiyohiko. "Mysterious Heavens and Chinese Classical Gardens." *Res* 15 (Spring 1988): 61–88.

A fascinating treatment of the complex spatial arrangements and abstract qualities of Chinese gardens, with special reference to the concept of Daoist paradise.

Qian Yun, ed. *Classical Chinese Gardens*. Hongkong: Joint Publishing Company, 1982.

Excellent photographs and brief descriptions of major gardens in China.

Jan Stuart is assistant curator of Chinese art at the Arthur M. Sackler Gallery and the Freer Gallery of Art. She has master's and undergraduate degrees in Chinese studies from Yale University and a graduate degree in Chinese art and archaeology from Princeton University.

Dream Visions of Transcendence in Chinese Literature and Painting

Wai-yee Li

Zhuangzi once dreamed he was a butterfly—joyous and carefree in being a butterfly. His heart's desires were fulfilled, and he did not know about Zhuangzi. All of a sudden he woke up, there he was, palpably and irrevocably Zhuangzi. He did not know whether he was Zhuangzi dreaming of being a butterfly, or a butterfly dreaming of being Zhuangzi. Between being Zhuangzi and being a butterfly there must be a difference. This is called the Transformation of Things.

—Zhuangzi, *Zhuangzi* (ca. 4th–3d centuries B.C.),
chap. 2, "Making All Things Equal"

This famous parable from the *Zhuangzi* points to a central ambiguity in Daoism. In this key Daoist text, which represents in part the thought of the historical Zhuangzi (ca. 369–286 B.C.), words like "dream" (*meng*) and "transformation" (*hua*) ring with the anguish of skepticism and mortality as well as with freedom for the spirit. The double perspective is sustained by a combination of philosophical wit, gnostic understanding, and an expansive imagination, qualities that made the *Zhuangzi* a constant source of inspiration for later Chinese thinkers and artists.

The shadow of mortality is just beneath the surface in the butterfly dream. If dreaming and wakefulness are equally valid forms of experience, so should life and death be similarly viewed. The grand acceptance of the flux between states of existence as the principle of the Transformation of Things prepares one for the ultimate transformation—death. Yet reckoning with death does not induce pessimism. The image of the carefree butterfly conveys, instead, a sense of spiritual freedom. The terror of death is transcended because its dissolution of the ego prepares for the harmonious union of subject and object. The reversal of the process of individuation in the dream state thus makes way for the joyous reintegration with the primordial unity of all things.

The dream experience as integral to the quest for alternate worlds that hold the promise of perfect bliss and freedom is a recurrent theme in Chinese literature. It appears in a wide

Detail, *Luo River Goddess.*
See figure 4a.

閑來隱几桃書眠夢入
壺中別有天彷彿吾
夷親面目大遷真訣得
親傳晉昌唐寅為
東原先生寫圖

Figure 1. Tang Yin, *Dreaming of Immortality in a Thatched Cottage*, ca. early 16th century, Ming dynasty. Handscroll, ink and color on paper, 11 × 40¹/8 in. Freer Gallery of Art, 39.60

range of writings, even as words like "transcendence" and "freedom" bear multiple interpretations. Freedom can mean philosophical detachment or unrestrained indulgence, and transcendence may take the form of freedom from the bondage of desire or freedom to pursue the object of desire. These two kinds of visions of bliss are epitomized, respectively, by the dream of Daoist reconciliation and the dream of the divine woman.

The Dream of Daoist Reconciliation

According to Daoist cosmology, the world is in constant flux. This phenomenon of transformation is a reminder of the limitations of the human condition—the impossibility of knowledge and the certainty of death: "For knowledge has to depend on something to be valid, and that which it depends on is never fixed" (*Zhuangzi*, chap. 6, "The Great and Venerable Teacher"); "The body is dissolved (transformed), and the mind is dissolved along with it. Is that not the greatest sorrow?" (chap. 2, "Making All Things Equal"). However, transcendence is within reach if one can delight in and harmonize with this process of change. Through a spiritual transformation, the capacious understanding of the Daoist sage encompasses opposites, which he recognizes as mutually dependent.

While philosophical Daoism

(*Daojia*)—the strands of thought associated with the *Laozi* (ca. 6th–4th centuries B.C.?), the *Zhuangzi*, and the *Liezi* (ca. A.D. 3d–4th centuries?)— envisions transcendence as a spiritual liberation bringing about reconciliation with the processes of change, religious Daoism (*Daojiao*)—a complex amalgam of folk, animist, and, later, Buddhist practices geared to ritual worship of the Dao—seeks to arrest or control such processes. Mystical, intuitive knowledge in the Daoist philosophy has its counterpart in magical, alchemical knowledge in the Daoist religion. Concomitantly, the spiritual transcendence of mutability in Daoist philosophical discourse becomes, in Daoist religious practices, a quest for the elixir of immortality that will pro-

long life and youth indefinitely.

Transformation and Immortality

In both philosophical and religious Daoism, there is an inherent paradox in the concept of perfect bliss. In the *Zhuangzi* we are told that "supreme joy is joyless." The sages are "passionless," "without selves," or "lost to themselves"; they are "withered wood and dead ashes," as if their sagehood is bound up with their sublime indifference to everything, including their very physical existence. By the same logic, supreme joy is tasted only by those who have risen above joys and sorrows, "those who will not allow themselves to be injured by their inclinations and aversions." In the butterfly parable the butterfly considers its desires fulfilled. Yet the butterfly state is at the same time a kind of death, for consciousness of self is obliterated: "He did not know about Zhuangzi." The fulfillment of desire paradoxically hinges upon the effacement of the desiring self.

This paradox is even more apparent in religious Daoism's conception of the immortal (*xian*). Here self-denial and detachment are but medial steps in the pursuit of a literal, physical immortality (*chengxian*) and the infinite gratification of desire. As first portrayed in the *Zhuangzi*, the immortal is decidedly otherworldly:

In the distant Guyi Mountain dwells a divine being. His complexion is pure as ice and snow, and he has the gracefulness of a virgin. He does not feed on the five grains. Wind and dew constitute his sustenance. He rides on clouds, reins in flying dragons, and roams beyond the four seas (chap. 1, "Free and Limitless Wandering").

From about the third century B.C., however, the idea of the immortal becomes increasingly this-worldly. When the First Emperor (reigned 221–210 B.C.) of the Qin dynasty and Emperor Wu (reigned 140–87 B.C.) of the Han dynasty sought the elixir of immortality, they were longing for the indefinite prolongation of life and worldly happiness. This spirit of worldliness is fully expressed in the belief, current by the second or third century A.D., that "when one person attains the Dao, his entire household ascends to heaven" and "even dogs and chickens followed suit."[1]

The Daoist immortal is, then, a curious mixture of the mundane and the magical. In many accounts Daoist paradises abound with gold, precious stones, and beautiful women. But in order to reach that realm the aspiring Daoist trains himself in austerity and abstinence. One may justly wonder what it means for Daoist immortals to enjoy plenitude and magical splendor if their emotions and desires have been refined out of existence. By the logic of sublime detachment, the immortal should be suspended in a void.

A handscroll called *Dreaming of Immortality in a Thatched Cottage* highlights the problems under consideration (fig. 1). The painting bears the signature of Tang Yin (1470–1523), but it has also been attributed to Zhou Chen (ca. 1470–ca. 1535), with whom Tang Yin studied. In this scroll there is a deliberate tonal contrast between the world of the dreamer and the world of his dream. Since the narrative handscroll is "read" from right to left, we seem to be following the process of how the dreamer experiences his dream. The right side of the scroll shows the dreamer in his cottage, surrounded by dense clumps of trees and solid rock masses. Asleep and reclining against a low table, he dreams of becoming an immortal. To the left, halfway between the dreamer and the end of the scroll, is an etherealized version of the dreamer suspended in the void. The dream image is smaller than the dreamer but still distinctly outlined. The image is relaxed, freely floating in midair, reminiscent of Zhuangzi's description of the nonaction (*wuwei*) of the Daoist sage as he "wanders in the realm of nonbeing."

Faint hills serve as background to the dream image. The diluted ink wash and aerial perspective in the left half of the scroll are a perfectly conventional way to represent distance.

The distant hills can be really present, or they can suggest receding forms perceived by the floating figure or dreamed by the sleeping figure. In this sense, there is no radical break between the dreamer and his dream world. The spiritual freedom symbolized by the dream image does not claim a transcendence beyond the world as immediately perceived, even as the butterfly does not claim ontological priority over Zhuangzi in the parable. The butterfly and the philosopher are equally valid manifestations of the Dao, and Zhuangzi's philosophical vision celebrates the freedom of the spirit in moving between these two states of existence. Similarly, in *Dreaming of Immortality*, we are impressed not so much by the revelatory significance of the dream image as by its resonant affinity with the dreamer.

At the upper left corner of the scroll is a poem by Bo Juyi (772–846):

In a moment of leisure, leaning against the
    desk, with books as pillows, I sleep.
I dream of entering the gourd—another
    heaven opens up.
It seems to be the very Face of
    Formlessness and Voicelessness—
The true secret of the Great Return is
    being passed on.

The idea of "a world within a gourd," just like the related concept of the "cave-heaven" (*dongtian*), implies both limits and limitlessness. The apparent self-contradiction is an attempt to be in and of both worlds, a means to "bring heaven down to earth."[2]

To create a world removed from ordinary experience yet potentially continuous with it, to juxtapose opposing realms that nevertheless admit seamless transition—this is the burden of a monistic philosophical vision of immanent transcendence. The Daoist idea of continuity between mundane reality and otherworldly transcendence is expressed on various levels. Fictional and pseudoscientific accounts of Daoist paradises are frankly preoccupied with material well-being. On a more philosophical level, it is the imagining, dreaming, or hallucinating subject that brings about the free transition between the present reality and the dream world.

This process is amply illustrated by a story in another important Daoist text, the *Liezi*, in which King Mu of Zhou (reigned 947–928 B.C.) visits regions of fantastic splendor through the aid of a Daoist magician. Upon King Mu's return to his earthly palace, his attendants tell him that his physical self has just been "sitting and lost in absorption." The magician then explains that the king has taken this journey in spirit and that the realm of magical splendor he beheld in his dream vision is actually no different from the palaces and parks that surround him every day.

"Spirit journey" or "roaming in spirit" (*shenyou*) can thus refer to the power of the imagination to transform. The world far removed from ordinary experiences may be literal and supernatural or may represent the roaming of the spirit as it contemplates nature or an object of art, in the process turning what is viewed into a kind of "dreamscape." In this context, it is significant that the characteristic movement of the Daoist sage or immortal is *you*, a word with connotations that include "playing," "roaming," and "wandering." A subgenre of

Chinese poetry devoted to this theme—*youxianshi* (poems on wandering [with] immortals)—often describes dream journeys to Daoist paradises. The idea of a spirit journey is of much wider application, however. Among other things, it bears on our understanding of nature poetry and landscape paintings. The aesthetic experience of writing, reading, painting, and viewing has a common basis in such spirit journeys.

You is, above all, a medial term; it describes the free and playful transition between states of being and levels of reality. In *Dreaming of Immortality*, for example, the setting of the dream image is both of this world and of the dream world. Dispensing with materiality in his conception of the world of the immortal, the artist still affirms the union of contraries in a journey of the spirit linking the dreamer's physical reality to his dream of immortality.

The medial function of *you* is also realized in the transition between dreaming and the wakeful state in the butterfly parable. In this sense, the quest of religious Daoism for literal, physical immortality and the Buddhist understanding of enlightenment as nirvana and the unequivocal liberation from desire and illusion (māyā) are both alien to the spirit of philosophical Daoism. As suggested earlier, the apparent moral of the butterfly dream is that Zhuangzi and the butterfly, self-consciousness and its negation, are equally valid manifestations of the Dao. By the same token, the moment a lucid intelligence expounds on the Transformation of Things is no less transcendent than the moment of undifferentiation and intuitive union with the Dao.

Nevertheless, there is a certain asymmetry between dreaming and the wakeful state in the parable. The butterfly is completely at one with itself; it does not ask whether it is Zhuangzi dreaming of being a butterfly or a butterfly dreaming of being Zhuangzi. It is upon waking that Zhuangzi poses the question, affirms the difference between the two states of being, and asserts that the difference defines two poles of a process of transformation, itself part of the great flux of all things. Zhuangzi is, in fact, aware of the irony implicit in the asymmetry. Between the experience of transcendence and the understanding or discussion of that experience falls the shadow. Transcendence is a form of forgetting, but philosophical reflection and language are rooted in remembering. Zhuangzi accepts the differentiating edge of philosophy and language with characteristic equanimity and playfulness: "Catch the fish and forget the net, catch the meaning and forget the words. Where can I find someone who has forgotten words, so that I may have a word with him?" (chap. 26, "External Things").

The Red Cliff Prose Poems

The interplay of the experiential and the discursive, self-reflexive dimensions in Zhuangzi's parable accounts for much of its subtlety and force. When these two dimensions are woven into a narrative, a complex psychological drama unfolds. Such is the case with the famous *Red Cliff Prose Poems* (Chibi fu) by the poet-scholar-statesman Su Shi (1037–1101). Infused with the spirit of Zhuangzi and similarly preoccupied with the themes of dream, transformation, and transcendence, these two sequential prose poems nevertheless seem to reverse the logic of the butterfly dream story. Instead of presenting philosophical understanding as the fruit of reflection consequent upon a dream experience of transformation and transcendence, in this poetic sequence the Daoist resolution is stated with lucidity and conviction at the outset, only to be followed by emotional tensions and an ambiguous dream encounter with a figure from the divine and numinous realm, a figure that embodies powers of magical transformation.

The *First Red Cliff Prose Poem* tells the following story: On the night of the seventh full moon of the year 1082, Su Shi and his friends are drifting in a boat on the Yangtze River beneath the Red Cliff. The poet's immediate response is an elation fraught with intimations of transcendence: We sailed "with gusto, as if leaning against the void and riding on the wind, not caring where we stopped. Adrift and floating, we seemed to be leaving the world of man to stand all alone, shedding our human forms to become immortals." His friend, however, is overcome with deep sadness at the mutability of all things and plays mournful notes on the flute.

Su Shi's friend is lamenting that a great hero is no more. He recalls that in 208, on the eve of the great battle that gave the Red Cliff its name,[3] Cao Cao (155–220), one of the greatest poets and political-military figures of his age, had leaned against the brow of his warship and composed lines of great pathos. Anticipating victory on the morrow, he had written of his grand aspirations and his melancholy over the limits of the human condi-

tion. The next day Cao Cao suffered a most unexpected defeat. Su Shi's friend mourns that glories and failures, the heroic and the pathetic—all vanish without a trace. If such is the fate of the great, the carefree enjoyment of the moment experienced by Su Shi and his friends must be even more ephemeral. "I grieve," says the friend, "that my life lasts but an instant, and envy the limitlessness of the Great River. How I wish to join the flying immortals in their distant wandering, embrace the bright moon and perish only when it does." The friend's plaint prompts Su Shi to express his vision of philosophical transcendence:

But do you really know the water and the moon? One flows forth and disappears, yet is never gone. The other waxes and wanes, yet never does grow or become diminished. For when seen from the perspective of change, heaven and earth last but the twinkling of an eye. But when seen from the perspective of changelessness, there is no limit to myself and the myriad things. What cause is there for envy. . . . Only the pure breeze on the river, and the bright moon in the mountains—the ears take them in as sounds, the eyes meet them as colors. There is no ban on drawing from them, no limit set on using them. This is the inexhaustible bounty of the Creator, and where you and I may find joy together.

The friend is consoled, and the prose poem ends on a happy note of carefree oblivion: "The growing dawn in the east stole upon us unaware."

The verbal echoes from the *Zhuangzi* in the *First Red Cliff Prose Poem* cast the poet as a philosopher with calm and unswerving gaze, seeking to be reconciled with negativity through rational understanding. The perceiving, imagining self has to go

Figure 2a. Detail, Qiao Zhongchang, *Second Red Cliff Prose Poem*, ca. 12th century, Southern Song dynasty. Handscroll, ink on paper, 115/8 × 2205/8 in. Nelson-Atkins Museum of Art, Kansas City, Missouri, Nelson Gallery Foundation Purchase

through mental somersaults to identify with the "perspective of changelessness" and rest content with the ever-present "pure breeze" and "bright moon." The dialogue form partly explains the poet's clarity and rationality. Su Shi sets out to enlighten, and his discourse is delivered with an audience in mind. Yet the resolution reached in this exchange, for all its sublimity, is no proof against the vagaries of poetic susceptibility. When Su Shi visited the Red Cliff three months later, he tested the limits of his philosophical erudition. This second visit is described in the *Second Red Cliff Prose Poem*.

The crux of the matter is this: Can anguish over mortality and the desire for escape to the realm of immortals (as voiced by Su Shi's friend) be reasoned away? Unlike the poet in the first poem, the poet in the second poem is no longer at pains to proclaim truths from the Olympian heights of philosophical understanding. Instead he tries to probe more deeply into the problems he set forth by confronting

raw experience and irrational fear. Three months have elapsed, and it is now early winter. The barren landscape forces upon the poet the very awareness of mutability for which he had earlier chided his friend: "How many days and months have passed, that mountains and rivers should change beyond recognition!"

The poet then leaves his companions to climb the Red Cliff alone. Nature, three months ago invoked as a source of solace, assumes a threatening aspect in this solitary encounter. The poet expresses his anxiety and fear in dense, allusive language: "Crouching upon rocks shaped like tigers and leopards, climbing gnarled trees like horned dragons, I reached upwards to the perilously perched nest of the eagles, and looked downward at the Dark Palace of the river god." The "perspective of changelessness" was grounded in understanding nature as orderly and constant, but here nature throbs with suppressed animation. It seems appropriate then that the poet's response should be one long, shrill, inarticulate cry, in contrast to his erudite philosophical exposition on the previous visit.

Among the paintings on the *Red Cliff Prose Poems*, a narrative scroll on the second poem by Qiao Zhongchang (active late 11th century to after 1126) is unusual in its combination of images and text to depict a narrative movement in spatial, temporal, and emotive terms. The poet's vertical ascent is represented in a horizontal scroll through huge rock masses that heighten the discontinuities of perspective and punctuate the development of the narrative (fig. 2a). Well aware of the unsettling implications of the metamorphic lines quoted above, in which the mood of nature is literally transfigured, the artist hid the three words "crouching," "tigers," and "leopards" ("crouching upon rocks shaped like tigers and leopards") in a dense clump of trees with tortuous, gnarled branches. The words are situated midway between the figure of the poet going up a mountain path on the right and the "perilously perched nest" on the left, which together mark the beginning and end of his solitary confrontation with nature (fig. 2b). The nest is perched above a body of turbulent water seen in bird's-eye view—a reference to how the poet "looked downward at the Dark Palace of the river god." The artist thus conveys the poet's fear and anguish by adopting his perceptual-emotive horizons and by carefully placing the written text in this section of the scroll.

The *angst* so powerfully portrayed through both words and images is quite different from the sadness expressed by Su Shi's friend in the *First Red Cliff Prose Poem*; it is more elemental and irrational. The experience of the numen inspires such intense fear and grief that the poet, utterly awestruck and disconsolate, has to withdraw. He returns, boards his boat, and sets it adrift, but any sense of

Figure 2b. Detail

返而登舟放乎中流聽其所止而
休焉時夜將半四顧寂寥適有孤
鶴橫江東來翅如車輪玄裳縞
衣戛然長鳴掠予舟而西也

Figure 2c. Detail

returning tranquillity (suggested in the scroll by the vast open space [fig. 2c], a deliberate contrast to the crowded images in the previous section) is disrupted by the cry of a solitary crane as it dives past the boat before disappearing to the west. The poet, returning home, then dreams of a Daoist in a fluttering, feathered robe, who asks whether his trip to the Red Cliff was pleasurable:

I asked his name, he lowered his head and did not answer. "Ah, now I know! Last night, the thing that flew past me with a cry, was that not you?" The Daoist looked at me and smiled. Startled, I woke up. I opened the door and looked for him, but I did not see anyone.

The dream as rendered in the scroll contains no suggestion of the preternatural (fig. 2d). Although the poet's couch does create the visual effect of a line separating the sleeping figure from his dream, the three dream figures seem to be simply sitting in front of the

couch. The squarely frontal view of the house adds to the sense of balance and calmness. To blur the distinction between dreams and wakeful life is consonant with the tendency, operative in most parts of the scroll, to convey the poet's psychic states by representing the world as filtered through his consciousness.

The final dream episode in the prose poem is an equivocal answer to the problem posed by the apparent inadequacy of the philosophical solution. Rational philosophical discourse fails to fortify the poet; he is completely powerless and overwhelmed in his solitary confrontation with a transfigured nature that seems to be full of fearsome creatures—tigers, leopards, and horned dragons. The transformation of the crane into the Daoist carries the metaphors of an animated nature one step further and seems to urge on the poet a magical understanding of the process of transformation that defies refuge in the "perspective of changelessness."

The phenomenon of change is itself changeless: to grasp this is to adopt the "perspective of changelessness." Here transformations are awesome, magical, and unpredictable; they are no longer simply various manifestations of a constant underlying principle. Yet the magical aura cannot really define a realm in which the poet may lodge his aspirations. Like an image in suspension and evanescent as a dream, the crane-Daoist can only point to a higher mystery. The final image in the scroll is that of the bemused poet leaning against the door, looking for his dream without finding any traces of the Daoist's presence (see fig. 2d).

In these examples from literature and painting the dream experience is linked to a philosophical vision of detachment and reconciliation. Literary and pictorial expressions of this sense of transcendence hinge on the juxtaposition of the world of common experience with a dream world where spiritual freedom and liberation from the anguish of mortality are possible. There is no radical disjunction between these two worlds; rather both literature and painting depict the transition from the mundane world to a higher realm of freedom and the concomitant promise of philosophical understanding and acceptance of mutability.

The Dream of the Divine Woman

In another Chinese poetic tradition the dream experience is associated with eros and emotional attachment, with plenitude and a vision of the ideal. The classic embodiment of this sensual and aesthetic gratification is a divine or divinely beautiful woman. In contrast to the mood of detachment and free play inspired by the "wandering between realms" in the Daoist vision of philosophical transcendence, the

Figure 2d. Detail

Figure 3a. Detail, artist unknown, *Luo River Goddess*, *baimiao* version (plain line drawing style), ca. 16th century, Ming dynasty. Handscroll, ink on paper, 9½ × 207½ in. Freer Gallery of Art, 68.12

dream vision of the divine woman is potentially tragic. Dominated by the dictates of passion, it follows a relentless logic of either-or. Loss and death are all too real.

The Chuci Tradition

The origins of this second tradition may be traced to the *Chuci*, a collection including songs and writings of the Chu culture (6th–4th centuries B.C.) and early Han (206 B.C.–A.D. 220) imitations of such works. The *Chuci* was first put together and designated as such by the Han exegete Wang Yi (ca. A.D. 89–158).[4] Roughly contemporaneous with the *Zhuangzi*, itself a product of the Chu culture, the *Chuci* is similarly impassioned and expansive in inventing imaginary realms. But while the solution of philosophical detachment and gleeful acceptance of the inevitable Transformation of Things is spun out in the *Zhuangzi*, the consolation of philosophy is not available to the shaman-

poets of the *Chuci* tradition, for whom the fusion of religious ecstasy and poetic inspiration leaves little room for philosophical reflection.

In the *Nine Songs* (Jiuge), the most explicitly religious and possibly the earliest stratum of the *Chuci* corpus, the trancelike, dreamlike spirit journey of the shaman-poet is a literal departure of the soul from the body in quest of direct communication with divine powers. The journey ends either in an all-too-brief encounter with the deity invoked or, as is always the case with goddesses and most notably the goddesses of the River Hsiang invoked in the third and fourth of the *Nine Songs*, in failure to meet with the divine being, futile waiting, and a melancholy return to this world. With *Encountering Sorrow* (Li Sao) by the poet Qu Yuan (ca. 340–278 B.C.), the quest for the goddess gains secular, political, and allegorical dimensions. The faithless goddess and the unsuccessful quest thus serve to accent the poet's fervent

Figure 3b. Detail

and uncompromising political idealism. These works plumb the depths of either-or: either ecstasy or despair, either mundane reality or the dreamlike otherworld holding forth the promise of magical transcendence.

The Prose Poem of Gaotang and the Prose Poem of the Goddess

The capricious goddess of the *Chuci* bequeaths to later literature a figure eluding the ordering functions of literary or philosophical structures. She beckons with the promise of a sensuous and aesthetic plenitude while remaining ultimately inaccessible. In two sequential prose poems attributed to Song Yu, the *Prose Poem of Gaotang* (Gaotang fu) and the *Prose Poem of the Goddess* (Shennü fu), the ambivalent divine woman makes her appearance again in a series of intractable transformations.[5] The *Prose Poem of Gaotang* is structured as an extended dialogue between Song Yu and King Xiang of Chu (reigned 298–

262 B.C.). It begins with Song Yu's account of the origin of the Gaotang Shrine, built to commemorate the previous king's dream union with the goddess Morning Cloud. When King Xiang desires to visit the shrine, Song Yu describes it with hyperbole, thus implying that the landscape is a metaphorical extension of the goddess and that visiting the shrine is tantamount to meeting her. In response, the king asks for a prose poem on the subject, and Song Yu's ready compliance produces the rest of the poem.

While the quest for the goddess is impassioned and hopeless in the *Nine Songs* and in *Encountering Sorrow*, in *Gaotang* the reality of the goddess is very much a function of Song Yu's rhetoric. The emphasis is on the process of her creation and the extension of her presence to natural phenomena through the poet's verbal magic.

Nevertheless, true to the spirit of her literary antecedents, Morning Cloud is

Figure 4a. Detail, artist unknown, *Luo River Goddess*, ca. 12th–13th centuries, Song dynasty. Handscroll, ink and color on silk, 9⁷/₁₆ × 122¹/₁₆ in. Freer Gallery of Art, 14.53-3

elusive. Her very name suggests transformation: "In the morning she manifests herself as clouds, in the evening as wind and rain." In the *Prose Poem of the Goddess*, the sequel to *Gaotang*, Song Yu describes his dream encounter with the figure called forth by his own words. But there is a striking contrast between the deliberate rhetorical manipulation of illusion in *Gaotang* and the tentative attempt to recapture an elliptical dream image in *Goddess*. The goddess in Song Yu's dream, implicitly identified with Morning Cloud, is seductive yet ultimately elusive. She comes unsolicited, but finally frustrates his desire for union, leaving him in profound melancholy at the end of the prose poem. The acts of dreaming, forgetting, and remembering endow the quest for the goddess with a new psychic dimension.

The Prose Poem of the Luo River Goddess

Another illustrious progeny of the elusive goddesses of the *Chuci* tradition is the Luo River goddess celebrated in Cao Zhi's (192–232) prose poem of the same name. This prose poem is the subject of many scrolls, including two in the Freer Gallery of Art, one from the twelfth to the thirteenth century painted in ink and color on silk, the other, from the sixteenth century, in ink in the plain line drawing style (*baimiao*). Although their exact derivation is extremely difficult to reconstruct, both are copies of an original composition probably datable to the latter half of the sixth century.[6] Since the earlier version is incomplete, I will refer to the *baimiao* version for the missing sections.

Cao Zhi's *Prose Poem of the Luo*

River Goddess is not, strictly speaking, about a dream experience. In the prose poem the spirit journey of the *Chuci* shaman-poet becomes a flight of the imagination, and shamanistic ecstacy, a ritualistic public spectacle, is transmuted into the intensity of a private poetic vision. This process of internalization was already under way in Song Yu's *Prose Poem of the Goddess*, to which Cao Zhi pays tribute in his preface. In linking the genesis of his work to Song Yu's dream poem, Cao Zhi suggests that the sudden access of the intense and private visionary experience bears comparison with dreams:

And then my soul is swayed, my spirit
    shaken,
All of a sudden my thoughts are dispersed.
Not noticing anything as I bowed down,
I raise my eyes to meet a splendorous
    vision.
I saw a beauty
At the side of the rocks.

Figure 4b. Detail

Figure 4c. Detail

It is a vision privy to the poet alone. When he tries to describe it to his coachman, he employs a series of metaphors to capture the aura of the goddess's expression and movement.

As for her form:
Alighting like the startled wild geese,
Supple as the roaming dragon;
Comparable to the glory of autumn
    chrysanthemum,
And the luxuriance of spring vines.
Evanescent as the moon concealed by thin
    clouds,
Fleeting as snow swept by swirling winds.
Viewed from afar,
She is brilliant as the sun rising amid
    morning clouds.
Seen when drawing near,
She glows like lotuses emerging from green
    waves.

The *baimiao* version of the *Luo River Goddess* renders these metaphors literally, arranging them around the goddess as iconographic attributes (fig. 3b). Such literalized metaphors emphasize the vision as the poet's own.

The poet, moved to deep longing for the goddess, unties his girdle jade and offers it to her as a pledge of love. The circumstances around this act depart significantly from its antecedents in the *Chuci*. In songs on the Xiang River goddess, the shaman-poet throws his thumb ring into the river after despairing of meeting the goddess. In *Encountering Sorrow*, the poet offers his girdle to Fufei, another name for the Luo River goddess, as a pledge of good faith. Fufei turns out to be fickle and faithless: "Though fair indeed she lacks all sense of Right Conduct." In these early examples the love pledge is a token of unswerving devotion in the face of a capricious goddess's whims.[7] By comparison, Cao Zhi seems, at

least initially, certain of the goddess's good faith:

Ah, the true excellence of that lovely lady;
Instructed in the *Rites*, conversant with the
    Songs.

Yet when the goddess offers her own jade pendant in return and points to the depths of the river to propose an assignation there, the poet is suddenly seized with fear and indecision:

Holding on to the hopes of ardent love,
I yet fear that this spirit may deceive me.
Moved by tales of how *Jiaofu* was
    confounded by faithless words,
I waver in uncertainty and melancholy.
Calming my features and stilling my
    thoughts,
I submit that I abide by rules of the rites.

This episode of exchanging gifts is of considerable psychological complexity (fig. 3a). In her study of the Luo River goddess scroll, Chen Pao-chen suggests that the attendant showing his back (*bei*) is a "visual pun" on the poet's irresoluteness and eventual turning back on his profession of love (*beixin*).[8] This visual pun may be yet another instance of how the artist externalizes the affective nuances of the situation through details in the setting of the figure experiencing intense emotions.

Rejected by the poet, the goddess departs in grief. The poet conveys the ambiguities of her receding figure through a cadence built on balanced oppositions:

Her movements conform to no constant
    pattern—
Now unsteady, now sedate.
Hard to predict are her starts and stops—
Now moving away, now turning back.

Her eyes flash fire in a backward glance,
Adding radiance to the glow of her
    jadelike face.
With words half formed yet unspoken,
She seems to breathe the fragrance of
    lonely orchids.

The goddess is defined by her liminal state. The syntax is reminiscent of Song Yu's *Prose Poem of the Goddess*, but here the inwardness is deeper and the emotions are more complex. The Luo River goddess loves the poet, yet, like him, she is constrained by higher imperatives.

The section from the earlier scroll begins with the image of the goddess half turning back and regretfully moving away (fig. 4a far right). She joins a host of mythical figures who are restoring order—the wind god gathers the wind, the river god stills the waves, and the half-animalian goddess Nüwa sings to the rhythm of the water spirit Pingyi's drumbeats. The mutual longing of the poet and the goddess threatens a confusion of the human and the divine, numinous realms. As order is restored, the boundaries are drawn afresh.

In the next scene the goddess is irrevocably installed in her mythic setting, driving a "cloud-chariot" pulled by six dragons (fig. 4b).

She cranes her white neck,
And turns back her clear brow.
Moving her red lips and speaking slowly,
Setting forth the Great Principle that
    governs conduct,
She grieves that the ways of men and gods
    diverge,
And regrets that we failed to meet in the
    days of our youth.
Raising her gauze sleeves to hide her tears,
Which nevertheless flow down her lapels
    copiously,

She laments that our happy meeting must
    end forever,
Mourns that, once parted, we will belong
    to different realms.
"There is no way to express my love—
I will give you these bright earrings from
    south of the [Yangtze] River.
Though I dwell in the depths of the Great
    Shadow,
My heart is pledged evermore to you, my
    Prince."

In contrast to the solitary goddess of Song Yu's dream, the Luo River goddess is presented along with her retinue, companions, and the paraphernalia of her mythic realm. She represents an entire world of wonders of which the poet is granted a glimpse—almost as a kind of compensatory consolation—as she departs. The final vision of the goddess is the most resplendent image in the scroll. Tantalizingly framed in a most dazzling setting, she is yet inaccessible and disappearing; even as she avows eternal devotion she speaks for a stern new order.

The loss of the goddess symbolizes the poet's sense of the insuperable gap between himself and his ideal. As in Song Yu's *Goddess*, the end of *Luo River Goddess* is suffused with a sense of hopeless longing. The last part of the earlier scroll shows the disconsolate poet absorbed in an all-night vigil (fig. 4c). The final image, preserved in the sixteenth-century *baimiao* version, is that of the poet's reluctant return to the world of men.

The Story of Su Xiaoxiao

The ambivalent divine woman realizes the ideal of sensuous and spiritual beauty; yet she may also be the harbinger of death. True to the spirit of the

Figure 5. Liu Yuan, *Sima Caizhong Dreaming of the Singing Girl Su Xiaoxiao*, ca. 13th–14th centuries, Yuan dynasty. Handscroll, ink and color on silk, 11 × 29 in. Cincinnati Art Museum, J. J. Emery Endowment and Fanny Bryce Lehmer Endowment

Chuci, the Luo River goddess obeys the logic of either-or: the ways of gods and men must diverge, and the goddess cannot be made to stay in this world. The other possibility is, of course, that the perceiving or dreaming subject will join the supernatural woman and leave the human world. Such is the import of the story behind the painting *Sima Caizhong Dreaming of the Singing Girl Su Xiaoxiao*, attributed to Liu Yuan (active 13th–14th centuries) (fig. 5).

Sima Caizhong (late 11th century) was a protégé of Su Shi, author of the two *Red Cliff Prose Poems*. In Liu Yuan's painting, the late fifth-century poet Su Xiaoxiao appears to Sima Caizhong as a young woman in a dream and recites a poem predicting their future union.

During the long period between her death and the event described here, Su Xiaoxiao had become a popular romantic figure. In the Tang dynasty, for example, Li He's (790–816) "The Grave of Su Xiaoxiao" (Su Xiaoxiao mu) powerfully evokes her mythic presence. He writes of the impossibility of binding love knots because no

one can bear to cut "mist-wreathed flowers," while waiting for the lover to come is futile:

Cold blue candle-flames
Strain to shine bright.
Beneath West Mound
The wind puffs the rain.[9]

Another Tang dynasty poet, Li Shen (780–846), relates the popular belief that music and singing could sometimes be heard emanating from Su Xiaoxiao's grave on stormy nights of wind and rain. The figure of Su Xiaoxiao thus evokes associations of a con-

suming passion unappeased in death and eternally expressed through music, which in Chinese literary tradition is sometimes linked to sensual excess and to access to the other world.

The right side of Liu Yuan's painting shows Sima Caizhong and his servant boy taking a nap. Wreaths of mist on the left announce the arrival of the spirit of Su Xiaoxiao. She holds a clapper in her right hand, a reference to the importance of music and poetry in her story. The earliest source for this story is *Hearsay at the Spring Sandbank*

(Chunzhu jiwen) by He Wei (1077–1145). According to this account, a beautiful young woman appears to Sima Caizhong in a dream and sings the following poem, entitled "Golden Threads" to him:

I used to live by the Qiantang River.
Flowers fall, flowers bloom,
Without regard for the passing of years.
The swallows are taking with them the
    colors of spring.
At the gauze window—how many bouts of
    yellow plum rain?

Later Sima Caizhong does in fact become an official in Qiantang. Behind his residence is the grave of Su Xiaoxiao, so his colleague Qin Shaozhang completes the dream song by adding a second stanza:

The horn comb is set at an angle in her
    hair, which is so like half-rising clouds,
Lightly marking time with her sandalwood
    clapper,
She pours her soul into the song of
    "Golden Threads."
The dream ends, colored clouds are
    nowhere to be found.
In the coolness of the night, the moon rises
    on the spring riverbank.

In her half of the song, Su Xiaoxiao sings of her melancholy at the passing of spring and the transience of beauty. In the second part, Qin Shaozhang writes about the beauty, pathos, and evanescence of the dream encounter. The mood of the song is intensely nostalgic.

In another version of this story, Sima Caizhong's susceptibility to visits from the spirit world is explained as the consequence of his inclination for writing "palace poetry" (*gongtishi*), a subgenre characterized by mildly erotic diction and an elaborate aesthetic surface. Associations with music and erotic poetry, with sensual excess and otherworldly transcendence, thus come into play here.

All versions end with Sima Caizhong's death. We are given to understand that he leaves this world for an eternal union with the spirit of the singing girl:

The boatman suddenly saw Caizhong boarding the boat with a beautiful lady. He was about to come forward to greet them, when a fire broke out at the rear end of the boat. He hurriedly reported it, only to find the family crying and lamenting [Caizhong's death].

Although in this instance death seems to be a kind of muted apotheosis, Caizhong has had to choose between this world and the dream world of Su Xiaoxiao. The logic is the relentless either-or.

Art as Transcendence

It is interesting to note that Chinese fiction and drama make frequent use of the dream motif, as if in tacit recognition of the dreamlike world one enters through the experience of reading a novel or watching a dramatic performance. The powerful aesthetic illusion, like the intensely lived dream, seems more real than life. The dream motif is often coupled with framing devices, a heightened sense of self-reflection, and implicit claims for art as transcendence. Woodblock prints illustrating fictional and dramatic texts, which became increasingly sophisticated and popular from the sixteenth century on, give ample expression to these ideas. In an illustration of the play *Romance of the Western Chamber* (Xixiangji), Chen Hongshou (1599–1652) depicts the austere simplicity of the world of the dreamer, in stark contrast to the elaborateness of his dream (fig. 6). The reclining figure, Zhang, has been forced to leave for the capital after his illicit love affair with Yingying came to light. Spending the night at a wayside inn, he dreams of Yingying's joining him and being forcibly taken away by a soldier. Since his deepest wish and greatest fear are realized in the dream, it seems entirely appropriate that the dream world should be so much more tangible and detailed than the real world. Perhaps the artist is making the same claim for the intensely experienced aesthetic illusion. In another illustration of the same scene by Min Qiji (ca. 1580–after 1640), the dreaming figure is dispensed with altogether. The dream vision emerges from a shell in the sea, an image evoking nostalgia, visionary intensity, and erotic longing.[10]

Throughout Chinese literary tradi-

Figure 6. Chen Hongshou, *Surprised in a Dream*. From *Romance of the Western Chamber* (Xixiangji), 1639, late Ming dynasty. Woodblock print, 7⅞ × 10⅛ in

賈寶玉神游太虛幻境

Figure 7. Wang Zhao, *The Spirit of Jia Baoyu Visits the Land of Illusion*. From *The Dream of the Red Chamber* (Hongloumeng), late 19th century. Woodblock print

tion tensions and transitions between worlds—between passion and the detachment born of enlightenment or between lonely melancholy and sensuous, aesthetic fulfillment—are combined and transformed in various ways. Classical tales such as "The World within a Pillow" (Zhenzhong ji, ca. 8th century) and "The Governor of Nanke" (Nankeji, ca. late 8th century), insofar as they articulate a final philosophical vision of detachment and spiritual liberation, may

seem closely related to Daoist themes. There is a crucial difference, however. Unlike the Daoist idea of roaming in spirit, these stories about a lifetime experienced in a dream privilege the moment of awakening, when the protagonist finally realizes the vanity of all things. In this sense, these stories are infused with the spirit of Buddhist transcendence, which also implies the logic of either-or. Here, however, the choice is not between the world of ordinary experience and the dream

警幻仙姑演曲紅樓夢

Figure 8. Wang Zhao, *The Fairy Disenchantment Performs the Dream of the Red Chamber*. From *The Dream of the Red Chamber* (Hongloumeng), late 19th century. Woodblock print

world but rather between ultimate enlightenment and the dream and illusion called life.

The theme of the dreamlike encounter with the supernatural woman is also played out in a variety of ways. The inaccessible woman to whom the poet directs his quest in the *Chuci* and *Prose Poem of the Luo River Goddess* rises to the status of a "symbolic other," that is, a being radically different from the perceiving subject and representing certain spiritual and aes-

thetic ideals. Often, however, the woman is merely an aesthetic object easily reintegrated into the existing social fabric. Many classical tales begin, for example, with a dreamlike encounter with a fox-spirit[11] or a ghost in the guise of a beautiful woman and end with the supernatural woman's attainment of human form and her union with the male protagonist. Through the supernatural woman the male protagonist can be in and of both the mundane world and the other world. This having-it-both-ways seems to show an affinity with the Daoist idea of free transition between realms of experience, except that the speculative energy and ironic edge of Daoism are lacking.

The grand exception to all these themes is the eighteenth-century masterpiece *The Dream of the Red Chamber* (Hongloumeng), also known as *The Story of the Stone* (Shitouji), by Cao Xueqin (1715–1763). In this work passion and spiritual freedom are paradoxically conjoined through the dream motif. In recapturing a lost world of splendor and exquisite sensibility, the author is living his most beautiful of dreams. Yet he frames this nostalgic dream with myths and allegories about the absurdity and the paradoxical truth of dreams: perhaps intense nostalgia tempered with irony makes for greater poignancy.

In chapter 5 the hero Baoyu dreams of a visit to the Land of Illusion, where the goddess Disenchantment guides him by the hand (fig. 7). She treats him to a musical performance of the "Twelve Songs of the Dream of the Red Chamber" (Hongloumeng qu shierzhi), which in cryptic language foretells the sad fate in store for the girls he knows and loves (fig. 8). Then she gives her sister to him in marriage. Disenchantment's avowed aim of disenchantment through enchantment, of warning against love through initiation into the art of love, of making Baoyu understand negativity through the plenitude of experience, makes her a highly ambivalent figure instrumental to a final understanding of the central paradox of the book: "enlightenment through love" or "the transcendence of passion through passion"

(*yichingwudao*). As both temptress and instructress, Disenchantment is linked to the Luo River goddess and other ambivalent divine women in Chinese literary tradition. At the archway to the Land of Illusion, where Disenchantment presides, is this couplet:

Truth becomes fiction when the fiction's true;
Real becomes not real when the unreal's real.[12]

The dialectic of reality and illusion, life and art, passion and enlightenment, nostalgia and knowledge are thus articulated in this most profound treatment of the dream motif in Chinese literature.

Wai-yee Li is assistant professor of comparative literature and East Asian studies at the University of Illinois at Urbana-Champaign. She received her Ph.D. degree in comparative literature from Princeton University in 1987. She has published articles on premodern Chinese fiction and the rhetoric of *fu* (prose poems) and is working on a book entitled *Between Worlds: Transformation and Transcendence in Classical Chinese Fiction*. She was recently elected a junior fellow in the Harvard Society of Fellows.

Notes

Unless otherwise indicated, all translations are by the author.

1. Sima Quian (ca. 145–90 B.C.), *Shiji*, 12.7a, 28.14b–15a; Ying Shao (ca. A.D. 140–206), *Fengxu tongyi*, Sibucongkan ed., 2.15b–16a. See also Yü Yingshih, "Life and Immortality in the Mind of Han China," *Harvard Journal of Asiatic Studies* 25 (1964–65): 80–122.

2. The idea of bringing heaven down to earth is a major theme of Wolfgang Bauer, *China and the Search for Happiness*, trans. Michael Shaw (New York: Seabury Press, 1976). For his discussion of the idea of "cave-heaven," see pp. 192–93.

3. The battle of Red Cliff, one of the most famous in Chinese history, was decisive in the consolidation of what came to be known as the Three Kingdoms (220–65). Cao Cao's entire fleet was burned, and in the glow of the raging fire the cliffs flanking the Yangtze River seemed to turn red, hence the name Red Cliff. Although Su Shi and his friend are adrift beneath a different Red Cliff, named for the reddish color of the rock, the geographical misattribution is of little consequence; what matters are the historical and literary associations.

4. A complete English version of the *Chuci* is available as *Ch'u Tz'u: The Songs of the South*, trans. David Hawkes (Oxford: Clarendon Press, 1959). The *Chuci* and the *Shijing* (Book of Songs, ca. 10th–6th centuries B.C.) represent the twin sources of Chinese poetic tradition.

5. Song Yu is an extremely nebulous figure, supposedly active in the Chu court in the third century B.C. Although the *Prose Poem of the Goddess* is attributed to him, its style indicates it was probably written sometime between the first century B.C. and second century A.D.

6. On the derivation of the two Freer scrolls, see Chen Pao-chen, "The Goddess of the Lo River: A Study of Early Chinese Narrative Handscrolls" (Ph.D. diss., Princeton University, 1987), pp. 280–85, 287–89. In this most thorough study of the subject Chen discusses various extant Luo River goddess scrolls and convincingly argues that the version in the Liaoning Museum, unique in its combination of images with words of the text to create a special rhythmic effect, is closest to the original.

7. David Hawkes suggests that the offer of jade may be a liturgical formula in shamanistic ritual. "The Quest of the Goddess," in *Studies in Chinese Literary Genres*, ed. Cyril Birch (Berkeley: University of California Press, 1974), p. 52.

8. Chen, "Goddess of the Lo River," p. 70.

9. Li He, "The Grave of Su Xiaoxiao," in *Poems of the Late T'ang*, trans. A. C. Graham (Baltimore: Penguin, 1965), p. 113.

10. The shell image may be an allusion to "Patterned Lute" (Jinse), Li Shangyin's (812?–858) enigmatic poem of love lost and remembered. See ibid., p. 171. Edith Dittrich suggests that the shell is a fertility symbol underlining the magic-erotic dimension of the dream. *Hsi-hsiang chi: Chinesische Farbholzschnitte von Min Ch'i-chi, 1640* (Köln: Museen der Stadt Köln, 1977), p. 60.

11. Chinese fox lore is based on the belief that the fox's habitat underground brings it into constant contact with the vital, cosmic yin essence. The cluster of associations includes therefore earth, womb, woman, yin essence, and supernatural powers of transformation.

12. Cao Xueqin, *The Story of the Stone*, trans. David Hawkes (Baltimore: Penguin, 1973–86), 1:55, 130.

Further Reading

Bauer, Wolfgang. *China and the Search for Happiness*. Translated by Michael Shaw. New York: Seabury Press, 1976.

Discusses ideas of happiness and transcendence in Chinese cultural history, considering such ideas in religious, philosophical, and sociopolitical contexts.

Birch, Cyril, and Donald Keene, eds. *Anthology of Chinese Literature from Early Times to the Fourteenth Century*. New York: Grove Press, 1965.

Contains A. C. Graham's translation of the two *Red Cliff Prose Poems*.

Cao Xueqin. *The Story of the Stone*. Translated by David Hawkes. 5 vols. Baltimore: Penguin, 1973–86.

A superior translation of what is by common consensus the greatest Chinese novel.

Chen Pao-chen. "The Goddess of the Lo River: A Study of Early Chinese Narrative Handscrolls." Ph.D. diss., Princeton University, 1987.

The most thorough study on the subject of early Chinese narrative scrolls.

Chibifu shuhua tejan (Exhibition of calligraphy and paintings on the Red Cliff). Taiwan: Palace Museum, 1984.

A comprehensive survey of paintings and calligraphy on the Red Cliff.

Chinese Rhyme-Prose: Poems in the Fu Form from the Han and Six Dynasties Period. Translated by Burton Watson. New York: Columbia University Press, 1971.

Contains a complete translation of the *Prose Poem of the Luo River Goddess*.

Ch'u Tz'u: The Songs of the South. Translated by David Hawkes. Oxford: Clarendon Press, 1959.

A complete translation of the *Chuci* accompanied by notes and introductory essays.

Chuang Tzu. *Chuang Tzu: The Inner Chapters*. Translated by A. C. Graham. London: Unwin, 1986.

A complete translation of the first seven chapters of the *Zhuangzi* accompanied by critical essays.

———. *The Complete Works of Chuang Tzu*. Translated by Burton Watson. New York: Columbia University Press, 1968.

A complete translation of all thirty-three chapters of the *Zhuangzi*.

Hawkes, David. "The Quest of the Goddess." In *Studies in Chinese Literary Genres*, edited by Cyril Birch, pp. 42–68. Berkeley: University of California Press, 1974..

A critical appraisal of the theme of the quest for the goddess in the *Chuci* and its transformation in Han *fu* (prose poems).

Hsi-hsiang chi: Chinesische Farbholzschnitte von Min Ch'i-chi 1640. Monographien des Museums für Ostasiatische Kunst. Band 1. Köln: Museen der Stadt Köln, 1977.

A reproduction of the Köln album of twenty-four prints by Min Qiji, with critical essays and commentary by Edith Dittrich.

Lawton, Thomas. *Freer Gallery of Art, Fiftieth Anniversary Exhibition*. Vol. 2, *Chinese Figure Painting*. Washington, D.C.: Smithsonian Institution, 1973.

Includes a discussion of the two *Luo River Goddess* scrolls in the Freer Gallery.

Schafer, Edward H. *The Divine Woman: Dragon Ladies and Rain Maidens in T'ang Literature*. Berkeley: University of California Press, 1973.

An account of how the divine woman, dragons, water, and power of transformation came to be linked in Chinese cultural history.

Chronology: China

Neolithic period	ca. 5000–ca. 1700 B.C.
Shang dynasty	ca. 1700–ca. 1050 B.C.
Zhou dynasty	ca. 1050–ca. 221 B.C.
Western Zhou	ca. 1050–ca. 771 B.C.
Eastern Zhou	770–221 B.C.
Spring and Autumn period	770–481 B.C.
Warring States period	480–221 B.C.
Qin dynasty	221–206 B.C.
Han dynasty	206 B.C.–A.D. 220
Three Kingdoms	220–265
Jin dynasty	265–420
Northern and Southern Dynasties	420–589
Sui dynasty	581–618
Tang dynasty	618–907
Five Dynasties	907–960
Song dynasty	960–1279
Northern Song	960–1127
Southern Song	1127–1279
Yuan dynasty	1279–1368
Ming dynasty	1368–1644
Qing dynasty	1644–1911
Republic	1911–
People's Republic	1949–

Coming in Winter 1991 *Games and Asian Art*

The origins of chess and backgammon in West Asia are examined along with equestrian ceramics in China and sumo wrestling—the ring, the ritual, and Japanese prints.

Back Issues

_____ Vol. I, No. 1 Fall/Winter 1987–1988
Inaugural Issue: Chinese Art
Milo C. Beach, Jonathan Chaves, Ann Yonemura, Thomas Lawton

_____ Vol. I, No. 2 Spring 1988
The Art of Eating and Drinking in Ancient Iran
Ann Gunter

_____ Vol. I, No. 3 Summer 1988
Art of India
Milo C. Beach, Stephen P. Huyler

_____ Vol. I, No. 4 Fall 1988
Pictures for the Islamic Book: Persian and Indian Paintings in the Vever Collection
Marianna Shreve Simpson, Thomas Lentz, Wheeler M. Thackston, Jr.

_____ Vol. II, No. 1 Winter 1989
A Lyric Impulse in Japan
William LaFleur, Ann Yonemura, J. Thomas Rimer

_____ Vol. II, No. 2 Spring 1989
Timur and Fifteenth-Century Iran
Glenn D. Lowry, David Bevington, Beatrice Forbes Manz, Lisa Golombek, Eleanor Sims

_____ Vol. II, No. 3 Summer 1989
Buddhist Art of South Asia
Conrad Hyers, Vidya Dehejia, Pratapaditya Pal

_____ Vol. II, No. 4 Fall 1989
Raghubir Singh's Photographs; Mughal Gardens
Raghubir Singh, Max Kozloff, James L. Westcoat, Jr.

_____ Vol. III, No. 1 Winter 1990
Japanese Ceramics, Crafts
Louise Cort, Amanda Mayer Stinchecum

_____ Vol. III, No. 2 Spring 1990
Ancient Chinese Music and Bronzes; Contemporary Chinese Folk Art
David Keightley, K.C. Chang, Kenneth J. DeWoskin, Nancy Zeng Berliner

_____ Vol. III, No. 3 Summer 1990
Yokohama Prints
Henry Smith, Julia Meech, Fred G. Notehelfer

_____ Check enclosed, payable to Oxford University Press
Please charge to my _____ MasterCard _____ VISA

Acct. # _____ Exp. Date _____

Signature _____

(Credit card order not valid without signature.)

Name _____

Address _____

City/State/Zip _____